Organizational Energy

PRAISE FOR ORGANIZATIONAL ENERGY

"Organizational Energy is a serious, rigorous and deep book. It is the best text I have read in years on management. The authors design a model and an approach to organizations considering the new challenges and thought paradigms of the 21st Century post-crisis society. A must read."
Rafael Barba, General Manager of Catalonian Clinics

"In these times of uncertainty, this methodology gives us the insight and tools to analyze and address the current challenges in our organizations. Central to the new model of conscious leadership lies the strength of the Organizational Energy System (OES). With its practical implementation, and ability to involve everyone across teams, we managed to get a much more efficient and aligned organization."
Joan Cañellas, CEO of Ficosa NAFTA

"I have a deeply appreciative to the authors for undertaking a titanic effort of synthesizing much of the available literature on cultural transformation processes. A paradoxical book: on one hand easy to read and accessible, on the other, extremely challenging for the reader in his ability to think outside the current schemes. A remarkable work as it forces the manager to ask questions about his/her leadership, and their actual ability to take the ideas into action ideas."
Jose Pablo Jaramillo Carvajal, executive at INTERNEXA

"Bernal, Cos and Tarré show how we can all harness the collective energy of our teams to fulfil our organization's potential in the new business paradigm. Organizational Energy is a fresh new book that should read by leaders everywhere."
Kevin Kruse, New York Times best-selling author, *We*

"Organizational Energy shows that in today's world the hard learning path is available to all human beings, and that we can turn the company into a new temple of mysteries in which to develop self-awareness. When we take the whole earth into account recognize the spiritual laws of the universe, the job and the company becomes sacred."
Joan Antoni Melé, Vice President of Triodos Bank

"The authors set out an innovative model to heal organizations and to achieve business prosperity. Far from establishing a theoretical construct of difficult application, they propose a practical methodology successfully tested. Definitely a highly recommended reading."
Joan Rafel, Corporate Director of People and Organizations at Abertis

"An innovative and visionary book. Highly recommended for everyone in the business world restless and interested in organizational change and evolution."
John Rigau, Legal Director of PepsiCo, Western Europe

"This book is a major contribution to the evolution of our views of organization and leadership moving us towards understanding them as Living Organizations. Boldly setting a new framework, the Organizational Energy System (OES)® modeled on the human energy system, the authors provide us with practical approaches to diagnose root causes and release blocked energy to open new pathways for innovation and business excellence. This is a must read book!"
Norman Wolfe, Chairman/CEO Quantum Leaders, author of "The Living Organization: Transforming Business TO Create Extraordinary Results"

Organizational Energy

7 pillars of business excellence

Enric Bernal (PhD),
Joan Cos,
Xavier Tarré

About Pinea3

Pinea3 is an international consulting and training firm specializing in conscious leadership, team development and organizational transformation using systemic and humanistic solutions and techniques. At the heart of our work is the belief that businesses is a force for good and that the future of a healthy and prosperous society lies in our leaders' ability to embrace the triple bottom line; people, planet, profit.

Organizational Energy, 7 Pillars of Business Excellence (2nd Edition).
Copyright © 2014 by Enric Bernal, Joan Cos, Xavier Tarré.
Copyright © 2014 by Pinea3 Living Organizations, S.L. All rights reserved.

Cover Design by Uffindell Group, London, UK
ISBN: 978-0-9905682-0-9

This book is the translation of a previously published book in Spanish: "*Energía Organizacional: 7 pilares de excelencia empresarial*" (Ed. Profit, 2012, Barcelona). When translating it, however, we have taken the opportunity to update it and to add a few more references relevant to the international English market.

CONTENTS

PREFACE

Yes!

You too are part of a great living organism undergoing expansion. Everything is energy, even organizations. Dip into the blue ocean of possibilities and create a more prosperous reality for you and your environment.

You can become an authentic leader who is aware of the new paradigm, and significantly help your business and your organization, a living system, to reach greater levels of excellence.

Together with the rest of human kind, you are part of a framework infinitely related to everything that exists and which, in turn, forms structures and organizations with their own lives and their own *organizational energy.*

It can be done!

ENRIC, JOAN AND XAVIER

INTRODUCTION

A few months ago the "low engine liquid sensor" of my old Volvo lighted up. In a mechanical system like a car, the dashboard alerts us that something within the system is not working as it is supposed to (this is the symptom). I bought antifreeze liquid and topped the expansion container up. As I had not addressed the problem that caused the light to go on in first place, in a few more weeks the low water indicator turned on again. I added liquid again so that the light would switch off. Recently, however, the "engine check" light turned on and the mechanic told me that the probable cause of the symptoms I had been observing (light indicators and engine misfiring) was that the head gasket was damaged. The root cause, however, was that sometime in the past the engine overheated above the normal temperature causing the head gasket to burn. Without entering more into the engine functioning details here, it's clear, that when something goes wrong we always have a choice: we could add water and temporarily address the "problem" or analyse the whole system and look for the underlaying bigger problem (e.g. the car has a burned head gasket and water is leaking from the radiator into the cylinders). From this example it is also obvious that we need to understand the car system in order to properly diagnose and fix the issues within the car.

Furthermore, if I expect my car to perform at its best all the time I not only will need to be able to identify the root cause of the problems, when they occur, but I will also have to regularly check and change its oil, break pads, tires, adjust the valves, etc. If I don't add oil and I burn the engine I will not be able to say: "*Oopps, sorry, let me add some oil now*" hoping that the car will continue functioning as before. I will have to rebuild my damaged engine. Nobody will doubt that preventive maintenance is necessary and that the more I proactively take care of my car, the better it will respond and last.

In a living system like our body, when we receive signals of malfunctioning we can equally address the symptom or look for the underlying causes. If I have a headache, I could take a pill because I cannot afford to lose one day of work or I can reflect about why I am having such a headache. Is it an excess of champaign or chocolate? A bad night sleep? A symptom of stress? Or something else which I don't know? As in a mechanical system I would need to know something about how the body system works or rely on an expert (a doctor or a healer). But what's more important is my willingness to look into my symptoms systemically… can I afford to just take a pill and continue as if nothing had happened?

As in a mechanical system, if we want our body to perform in a half marathon race, in a tennis match, in a chess championship, or at work, we will have to make sure we have all the energy that such efforts entail. So probably we will insure we sleep enough hours, we eat properly and we exercise regularly. And if we break a ligament (hopefully not playing chess!) we will have to heal our system, which like for a car, it will inevitably take longer and it will be more painful than if we had watched our overweight, had trained more or improved our running technique. In summary, we need to invest in our health (preventive actions) more than reactively curing the problems.

In organizational systems the exact same philosophy applies. First of all, we frequently address the symptoms, not its causes. If our sales are dropping, we may address the issue with an increased marketing budget or with additional pressure to our suppliers to reduce costs instead of evaluating other potentially malfunctioning aspects of our system. For instance, we could ask ourselves: Are our products and services adding real value to the market (as they used to)? Are our different business units cooperating for the common good? Is there alignment around our vision? Are people engaged and motivated? Do we have the right leadership? Etc. In organizational and business settings, once again, the same systemic principles apply. Do we understand our organization as an interconnected system with symptoms of malfunctioning or are we addressing them in isolation?

And as in the previous systems, if we expect our organization to perform at its best, we will need to assure that there is plenty of positive energy in the system. And we will need to invest in strategy and people before needing them. People's commitment and level of engagement is something that employees and collaborators grant to the organization, is not something we can buy. Like breaking the engine or a ligament, if we decide to ignore our corporate values "for a while", maybe until the crisis is over, we will not be able to have a quick bounce back. We will need to invest in re-building our damaged system, which is much costly than investing in preventive maintenance.

If you are interested in exploring questions like:

- How do we need to look at our organizational issues to be able to address the real causes instead of patching the symptoms?
- What can we do to have our workforce energetic, resilient and engaged?
- How can I develop and grow my organization so that it will be able to "run an iron-man"?
- What is the "preventive maintenance / medicine" for an organization in order to avoid future system breakdowns?
- Why systemic thinking should prevail -over the mechanistic one- to have sustainable success in our economy and our organizations?

Then, continue reading.

Why is this book needed? Why now?

In the preface above we started with a positive and empowering note about what we could become and what are our possibilities, as individuals, as organizations and as a collective. We, however, are somewhat disappointed at the rate our society has been evolving in the past few years. We have seen institutional failure in many geographies and the accentuation of global unwanted results such as hunger, poverty, pandemic illnesses, violence and terrorism. We are also "getting into debt" with our planet by consuming 50% more resources than the planet is able to produce, causing serious consequences like climate change and the extinction of species and communities. It is a period of many challenges and many changes at all levels. We believe that the way we understand, lead and manage our organizations can have a dramatic positive return into the world and into the system we live in.

No doubt that we have also witnessed positive changes in the business paradigm towards more sustainable and complete models of engaging people and using our limited resources. Yet, we lack new tools and models for leading and managing.What helped us get to where we are, may not be what we need going forward. Business (and organizational) management as we know it today was developed in the 19th century and needs to be updated. Many organizations are sick and need help to heal. We need new formulas and tools adapted to the 21st century, a period with very different challenges. We require new models of cooperation in politics and in business management to help us improve collectively. As Gary Hamel describes in his book *"The future of management"*[1], the principles of what we call 'modern *management*' are over a hundred years old. We need more complete and holistic models, which take people into account and consider their feelings, understand their work motivations, respect their values and also value the environment where they develop.

As explained before with the car and the body examples, many times management practices are centered on fixing problems reactively, more than investing in preventing them proactively. Even leadership development -at individual, group, or organizational level- is often funded when the person, the team or the collective has shown signs of malfunctioning. New models and tools are needed that focus on healing (or maintaining health) more than curing.

In this book we propose a change in perspective and the adoption of a more systemic view of the world and the universe. Dalai Lama says that "the mechanistic understanding of the world led to the Industrial Revolution, in which the exploitation of nature became the standard practice" [2]. The Systemic view, on the other hand, looks for understanding and comprehension among people and interest groups. It does not blame the individual for behaviors that rise from the organizational structure and culture. Instead, it promotes awareness and brings consciousness into the organization. In his book "*The Theory-U*"[3] Otto Scharmer tells us that at this point in history we need a new awareness and ability for collective leadership to face challenges in a more deliberate, strategic and conscious way. Only through the development of this ability will we be able to create a future with more opportunities for everyone. As Einstein stated, "No problem can be solved from the same level of consciousness that created it".

But we are not trying to demonize the mechanistic view as it was a necessary step in our evolutionary journey. What we are defending is that, in 2014, our social consciousness and wisdom has thankfully increased and the mechanistic view has become old, it doesn't serve us well anymore.

In this book we also present a methodology for organizational change that makes us more aware of our organizations as living systems. We have developed an analogy between the human energy system and the Organizational Energy System (OES)®, which allows us to understand and treat companies (public and private) in order to improve their health and productivity. If we accept that organizations are living organisms we will be interested in understanding how can we proactively focus on nurturing and maintain their health, instead of patching its symptoms and curing its diseases.

Our experience as executives, entrepreneurs and consultants for more than 20 years around the world has led us to develop a systemic methodology that works with the energy of organizations to improve their levels of excellence, health and prosperity. This methodology meets the challenges of the new era, transforming our organizations and healing their structures and outdated belief systems.

There are many authors who deserve recognition for their contributions to developing a better world and who are calling for substantial changes in how our organizations are managed: Barrett, Blanchard, Dilts, Hamel, Kofman, Scharmer, Senge, Trompenaars, Wilber and a long list of thought leaders. We join them and suggest a new and practical way to heal our companies through the Organizational Energy System (OES)®.

The world needs a new form of leadership and more conscious co-operation in order to co-create a more prosperous future for mankind.

How to read this book

It was our wish to create a highly practical book and for this reason we have included many examples. At the same time, we wanted to provide documented evidence of the theories and philosophy behind our transformational methodology. The first two parts focus on more abstract concepts. Later in the book, these are applied to the most practical problems of our everyday business world.

In Part I of the book (*The reality of the 21st century*) we present the current context as we see it. We talk about social and environmental changes in the world as well as the changing business paradigm that we are witnessing.

In Part II (*The Meta-Model of Conscious Leadership*), we interpret these changes and concepts and classify them into a model. The model allows us to apply these concepts to the corporate world and the non-profit sector for organizational healing.

In Part III of the book (*The Organizational Energy System (OES)®*), we present our systemic model of 7 pillars for business excellence in detail. We stress the importance of considering the organization as a living organism through a wide variety of examples.

In Part IV (*Pinea3 Methodology®*) we reveal our methodology for organizational change with examples and real cases. In this section, we also provide a questionnaire for self-diagnosis of the SMEs and teams.

In Part V of the book we introduce *The MRW case study*. We explain how our methodology was successfully applied in 2011 to the MRW firm at the request of the Martin family, a good example of conscious leadership.

We would like this book to be useful to its readers and we understand that different people may have different priorities, interests and reading styles. We organized the book content in an way that made sense to us, going from abstract concepts to practice. However, you may prefer to start with the practical application and only afterwards look for the necessary theoretical support in previous chapters. If you are looking for an executive and practical approach, you may go directly to Parts IV and V of the book. Starting in Part I for you may be too slow and theoretical. On the contrary, if you are interested in knowing the origins of our methodology and our interpretation of the challenges of this new era, you may want to start at Part I and II. And if you are interested in the new management concept of the Organizational Energy System (OES)®, the "Organizational Chakras", look at Part III. You don't even have to agree with all of our points of view to be able to take advantage of the OES model. We hope you like it.

PART I

THE REALITY
OF THE 21ST CENTURY

- The Turn of an Era
- The Planet Earth in Transformation
- Social and Environmental Sustainability
- Towards a New Paradigm
- Evidence of Change

The Turn of an Era

The development of modern civilization rests on a series of transformative discoveries such as the printing press, the railroad, electricity, the combustion engine, the telegraph or the cinema. In the last century we have experienced the greatest advances in the field of information and communication technologies. Changes like the television, the microprocessor and the Internet have defined our current social and economic reality. In this way, we have moved from the industrial era to the information era, which has made multichannel communications possible anywhere in the world, thus facilitating economic globalization.

The industrial era solved the problem of production capacity. Based on a mechanistic understanding of the world, there was a period characterized by a huge leap in productivity and efficiency. However, this mechanistic view, which considers the production process just as a series of inputs or materials being transformed to produce specific results or products, is being questioned today.

Since the middle of the last century there have also been a number of social and demographic events that have revolutionized our existence. In this chapter we quickly expose some of the most important changes that are transforming our world.

At a social level, the entry of women into the labor market is probably one of the major drivers of change in our society. Some writers have pointed out that the 21st century is, and will be, a much more feminine century than the last one. Feminine values (representative of wider values of femininity such as respect, cooperation, empathy and care) are essential for promoting economic and social development in our planet in a sustainable way.

Another decisive factor in the socio-economic changes of the recent years is the exponential growth of the world population. During the 20th century the world population rose from one billion people to almost seven billion, an unprecedented growth. It is expected that by 2050 there will be ten billion people sharing the planet. This fact alone can destabilize humanity unless we change our way of thinking about the resources of our planet.

Not only is the world population growing at great speed, but there is also an increasing number of people moving from one country to another. These migratory movements from poorer to more developed countries have been and continue to be the cause of much social stress across many countries. Organizations, both public and private, have also seen growing cultural diversity in their structures, which they are struggling to manage within their classical management mentality.

The most recent element of the socio-demographic changes in our society is the inverted age pyramid in the more developed countries. The richest countries are fighting against the progressive aging of their respective populations, due to the low birth rate and an increase in average life expectancy. Our aging population will necessitate changes in pension policies. Organizations may experience a lack of qualified professionals for key positions and different generations of workers with diverse values and ways of understanding life and work.

The debate about the retirement age has already been reopened in Europe, thus, intergenerational management will become increasingly important in organizations. This means that professionals will cover spans of more than 40 years actively working for a company. Each generation is characterized by a set of values and, consequently, a different vision of the world, which poses a special challenge for the management of such heterogeneous groups.

Another aspect of the aging population in the developed countries of Europe is the competitive impact of the retirement 'bulge'. The generation of the "*Baby Boomers*" began to retire in 2008. In the coming years the biggest firms are going to need well-structured succession planning. *Goodrich*, for instance, a manufacturer of engines for the aerospace industry, saw one thousand engineers retired in 2011 in their San Diego (California) plant alone. A mass exodus of seasoned staff may result in a loss of critical knowledge and expertise in an organization.

There are countries that show more or less healthy age pyramids. India, for example, will have a balanced population growth over the next 40 years that can help the country become a leading economy in the near future. On the other hand, countries like Germany, Italy and Spain have age pyramids that look more like a spinning top than a pyramid or, worst of all, like an upside down pyramid. Immigration can help to solve this problem, as long as those who arrive are suitably qualified for the organizations' needs. But large-scale immigration brings its own issues and challenges.

On a different note, spiritual values are being questioned by the 'down-to earth performant business world'. Since the nuclear era of the 1940s, our work, our environment and, ultimately, our lives, have developed at breakneck speed, unlike our spiritual understanding. The accelerating rate of successive changes in the world places great strain on an individual. In order to stay grounded, the individual needs to have very clear and deep-rooted values. Consumerism can be tempered with a spiritual perspective, and people, who can adapt to the pace of our changing society without losing that perspective and who are committed to future generations. At the same time, the traditional religious orders have lost followers by not adapting to or addressing the emerging challenges facing our society. For this reason, there has been a growing skepticism towards the role of religious doctrines and many people have started to look elsewhere for new answers to the fundamental questions: the meaning of life, our purpose, the meaning of happiness.

All of these tensions, challenges and massive changes have produced a visible symptom recently: The economic crisis, which began in 2007 and is not yet over in some countries in 2014. Yet, it is not just a crisis of the economic and financial world. It is one of the most visible results of the change of era we are experiencing, which will make us aware of the changes society needs. Many authors have called it a crisis of values. In fact, this and other problems affecting the European Union at present (excessive debts in Southern Europe countries or the lack of cohesion and interstate leadership) are opportunities to increase our global consciousness and to learn about our behavior as a society. If we do not get to the roots of the problems or if we fail to understand the underlying causes, we can expect the same symptoms to reappear.

No doubt the impressive social and economic advances of the 20th century have greatly contributed to the development of humanity; a leap that has never been possible before. But the changes have occurred at an exponential rate and many of them, as we have pointed out in this chapter, have led us to an unsustainable situation when given close scrutiny. Nothing in human history is comparable to the scale of changes we are currently facing, and rather than living through an era of change, it looks like we are living the turn of an era.

If the changes suggested above are not sufficient to persuade us that we are at a point of inflection, we will see how our own planet responds with the scientific facts, perfectly measurable and daunting in their magnitude.

The Planet Earth in transformation

There has been a lot of talk recently about climatic change and the degradation of the ecosystem. In fact, these transformations have been occurring and been researched for many years. In 1865 John Tyndall postulated that gases like steam from water and the CO_2 in the atmosphere retain heat. By 1895 Svante Arrhenius was predicting that increases in CO_2 in the atmosphere from the use of fossil fuels would cause global warming. The concentration of CO_2 in the atmosphere has been growing exponentially since the middle of the 20th century.

The danger lies in interrupting the circulation system of the oceans, which prevents the global warming of the planet. On average, the earth has already grown warmer by 0.74°C, mainly since 1970, and the predictions are that at the end of this century temperatures will have increased by between 2 and 4.5°C. According to the analyses, we can expect the sea level to rise by 1 meter by the year 2100. This will be enough to displace

100 million people in Asia, 14 million in Europe, and 8 million in Africa and South America. Some scientists speak about critical moments of inflection. If these occur, they may destabilize whole ecosystems that have survived for thousands of years, with the potential risk of the sea level rising by an even higher number of meters [4]. This may sound like science fiction or a trite Hollywood movie, but it would be consistent with what we know happened during climate changes in the past; changes such as the sudden global warming after the glacial period that took place in only a few decades.

In order to prevent disasters of this type, scientists say we should keep global warming under 2°C. To do this, we must dramatically reduce the gas emissions that are causing climatic change. According to estimates, gas emissions in 2050 should be 80% less than the levels in 1990 [4].

The main problem lies in the fact that the gases we emit stay in the atmosphere for centuries before being eliminated. Consequently, the fairest way to compare the contribution of the different countries to climatic change is not only assessing the *current* emissions of gases per capita from fossil fuel. A fair scheme must also take into account the long history of previous emissions. The USA and Europe contributed to the CO_2 emissions a 30% and 28% respectively during the 20th century. The Asian countries, less industrialized but with very high growth rates at this moment, are only responsible for 12% of the historic emissions [4]. The majority of these countries continue to invest in energy projects based on coal, although there are many other options available. The dilemma that we have to face is how to cover our energy needs with greater input from renewable energy.

There are solutions based on the concept "the one who pollutes pays". But the most important and difficult issue is mutual trust and co-operation between the nations, because of the huge investments needed. In 1995, the Intergovernmental Expert Group on Climatic Change published a report that showed a wide scientific consensus on ratifying global warming as a real phenomenon, while acknowledging that there were still many details to analyze. The report included the following joint declaration from more than 2,500 economists, including several Nobel Prize winners:"The most efficient method to slow down climatic change is through open policies based on market principles. The world will only be able to reach its climate goals with a minimum investment by using collaboration strategies between the nations like, for example, the search for an international agreement for the emissions trading."

The 1997 Kyoto protocol was the first time the most industrialized countries of the world agreed to establish goals for reducing emissions in the 2008-2012 period. However, many countries have not reached these goals. For example, in Spain, according to a study by the Institute of Technological Investigation (IIT) of the University Pontificia Comillas of Madrid in 2009, the total volume of gas emissions (including CO_2 and other greenhouse effect gases) is 63% higher than in 1990. Under the Kyoto Protocol, Spain's commitment in 2012 was to emit only 15% more than in 1990 – a huge gap.

The Kyoto Protocol ran out in 2012 and new objectives need to be established. At the climate change conference that took place in Bali in 2009, it was pointed out that the industrialized countries should establish 2020 objectives for reducing emissions of around 25% and 40 % with respect to the 1990 levels.

In August 2009 the analysts of the U.S. Military and U.S. intelligence acknowledged that climate change posed a threat to national security. One of the biggest organizations in the world, the American military service is preparing to face up to the consequences of climatic change. In public statements, their spokespeople said that they are not only concerned about the direct consequences of climate change (such as the rise in the sea level and the melting ice caps), but even more so about the side effects of climate change. These were listed as water shortage, floods, hurricanes, hunger, massive migrations, pandemics, social discontent, political instability and emergency evacuations.

In late 2009 at the Copenhagen Climate Change Conference, the U.S., China, India, Brazil and South Africa drew up a document stating that climate change was one of our greatest current challenges and that measures should be taken to prevent global warming above 2°C. Unfortunately, the document did not impose any legal obligation to reduce CO_2 emissions. Notwithstanding this, the proposal was rejected by the participating countries. During 2010, partly due to this disappointment, a total of 138 countries signed an agreement stating that they would reduce their emissions in the future. And at the 2011 Conference in Durban, South Africa, a new treaty was signed to limit coal emissions. On this occasion, the conference drew up a legal document to include all the participating countries, which will be prepared for 2015 and will come into effect in 2020. Progress was also made by the creation of a fund for the climate change (*Green Climate Fund*), which will provide one hundred billion dollars a year in order to help poor countries adapt to climate impacts. The president of the conference Maite Nkoana-Mashabane declared the agreement a success. However, the scientific community and environmental groups warned that the agreements were not sufficient to prevent potential catastrophes if global warning exceeded 2°C.

The truth is that nobody really knows exactly what will happen on climate change. But it is clear that the world's ecosystem is being seriously degraded by our misuse of the resources and that there is a limit to how long this situation can last. There are more examples every day. As Director of *Oxfam International* Ariadne Arpa mentions, more than 12 million people only in East Africa are facing hunger and water shortage. In some areas, the population is experiencing the worst drought in 60 years. Hundreds of animals have died and the price of food has rocketed. Millions of lives in countries like Somalia, Ethiopia, Kenya and Uganda are in danger [5].

It is clear that the solution will come through technological advances in renewable energies. Countries like Germany, Spain, Denmark, the U.S., India and China continue to invest heavily in wind energy. Spain and the U.S. make industrial scale investments in solar energy, in bio fuel from agricultural waste like methane, in extremely efficient electric vehicles and in high-speed electric trains.

At a personal level we can also become active. Increased awareness means we can no longer plead ignorance. We have to change both our consumption habits and our behavior. In fact, we have to redesign our lifestyle.

At an organizational level, there is also great potential for improvement in efficient energy use. This is true in nearly all sectors, from heavy industry to transport, construction or consumer goods. It is estimated that with product redesign and modifications not only can product costs be reduced, but also the energy used will be 30% to 80% less.

To summarize, all the objective indicators show that we have reached a point where we must radically change our way of life and our behavior. Otherwise, at this pace, the human race will probably disappear in the not too distant future. Perhaps it helps to remember that if all the insects on Earth disappeared, the fauna and the flora would completely disappear as well. But if the human race became extinct, there would be an abundance of life on Earth again. It is not about dramatizing and blocking in front of such scenarios. Quite the contrary, it is about ringing the alarm bells and doing something about it. We are at countdown time. We must face the huge challenge globally in order to build a new reality.

An optimistic approach of this challenge, characteristic of a new era of humanity, is turning it into an opportunity for new businesses. This is a win-win situation: there is a big market opportunity and, moreover, the new ventures will help us solve problems and change an economy based entirely on material benefits into one that is more sensitive to real human needs and nature. The next chapter explores this idea in more detail.

Social and environmental sustainability

In the last two chapters we have discussed a series of problems that have been accumulating over the course of recent decades. At this point we need to ask the questions: "Who is in the best position to face these world-scale challenges?" "Is it the political leaders who will get us out of this predicament?" It would not be fair or reasonable to assume they will be able to do this on their own. We believe instead that businesspeople and large companies can have a more effective impact on the social and economic transformation required at this point in time.

However, the scale of transformation makes it a strategic issue involving great responsibility, which requires new leaders who are up to the challenge. Consequently, it is necessary for Corporate Social Responsibility (CSR) to stop being at the margin of business leadership considerations and make a move to the centre; to be given priority from the board of directors downwards. We propose that social responsibility should be part of the true essence, the business objectives and the purpose of any organization. This is the real challenge as it is the best solution to speed up global change. The key lies in making our society (as consumers) more conscious. Organizations need thousands of new leaders who understand the need for businesses to stop prospering at the expense of the broader community and who have the vision and the courage to carry it out.

There are increasingly more consumers who want to show loyalty to brands that mean something more than just a material product or service. All of us can observe first-hand how the economic fragility and the degradation of the environment affects everyone alike. We see hope in the many consumers that are now ready to single out products or services that, in addition to meeting a basic need, also show true respect for our social and environmental milieu. Studies have shown that positive CSR information has lead to significant increases in product sales and refferals while negative CSR news has lead to boycott a company's products [6]. According to Dutch consulting company *Between-us*, specializing in Corporate Social Responsibility since 1997, companies considered highly sustainable already outperform their unsustainable rivals by 4.8% in share price performance. Evidence exist that people's consumption patterns are influenced by corporate social responsibility efforts, however, there are many implications which are not yet clearly defined.

At the 1999 World Economic Forum in Davos (Switzerland), the Secretary General proposed a "World Treaty" between the United Nations and the business world. The World Treaty asked the companies to internalize, support and put into practice a series of fundamental values relating to human rights, labor norms, the environment and the fight against corruption. He proposed ten key principles [7]. In 2012, the United Nations Global Compact continues to be the greatest global sustainability initiative in the business sector, a synonym of business responsibility.

Sadly, the tactic of many businesses has been to paint themselves in a new 'green' image to be more attractive to the market. Initial confusion in a rather immature market enabled some to take advantage of the consumer and to use CSR more as a brand marketing strategy than as a genuine end in itself. This attitude has undermined many potentially useful projects. But consumers have now become savvier and this tactic has become less and less acceptable, discrediting the brands that sponsored them. And this message is getting through to major businesses. Taking Corporate Social Responsibility seriously and providing the resources needed is a good start for any strategic plan that aims to manage an organization beyond solely short-term financial gain —a strategic plan that also contributes to the making of a new economic system, more in harmony with nature and ourselves.

Surveys recently carried out by organizations such as *McKinsey, IBM, PWC* and the *North American Management Association*, have all highlighted that Corporate Social Responsibility will become a central issue in the companies' business strategy [8]. The meaning of corporate social responsibility will also change. The concept is often understood as corporate actions that have a social impact, without necessarily including the need for sustainable environmental policies. These two concepts are merging and when we talk about Corporate Social Responsibility here, we mean business policies that address both social and environmental sustainability.

Companies such as *Inditex, British Telecom, Danone, Interface, Novo Nordisk, Unilever or Vodafone* are already recognized as leaders in such policies. Today there are few large companies without some type of sustainability plan. And in recent years, there has been a growing number of forward-thinking, small-to-medium enterprises (SME) adopting broader strategic approaches to sustainability. An example of this is *MRW*, to which we dedicate the last part of this book.

In his article *"Eight reasons why social and environmental sustainability will change management"*, Hopkins, Editor in Chief of the *MIT Sloan Management Review* [9], states that all organizations will have to face up to social and environmental sustainability, either in a conscious, proactive way or in a reactive, unplanned one. Companies such as *Nike, Unilever, Wall-Mart, Boral Limited, Rio Tinto* and *Chevron* have had experience in this. Before defining a strategic position of sustainability, they had to face situations that made them approach sustainability reactively. The article shows that companies that are ahead of the "clash" against sustainability will face less traumatic internal changes than those that postpone change until there is no other alternative.

But sustainability should not be regarded as some business evil that we must reluctantly embrace. In the *Business of Sustainability* research project, organizational leaders and business management theorists found that companies following sustainability strategies experience increased staff motivation and productivity. The article also highlights other positive results flowing from the incorporation of social and environmental sustainability into the company's strategic agenda. Such organizations stop thinking of themselves in a bubble and are prompted to consider the whole ecosystem where they operate, which sheds unexpected light on some areas of the business model and also yields unexpected business model improvements. The report quotes President of *Coca-Cola* Jeff Seabright: "The sustainability agenda offers business perspectives that were not obvious perhaps at the beginning of the journey."

Laura Quinn and Jessica Baltes from the Center for Creative Leadership published a study with 36 organizations and reported that, according to the leaders, the top three advantages to adopting a triple bottom line approach are increased revenue and market share, increased employee retention and increased community support [10]. A *BusinessWeek* study [11] indicated that employees working for organizations with a strong Corporate Responsibility programs were happier and more satisfied with their jobs and had the companies had longer retention rates. In addition, a Stanford University study [12] shows that MBA graduates will take a lower annual salary to work for a 'responsible' company.

The more advanced companies are already talking about 'responsible innovation' in their products and/or services. They have abandoned a narrow approach that focused only on elaborating their products to drive more consumption. Now they are asking a more profound question –is our product good for our customers? By adopting this wider eco-system view, they open up to new ways to gain efficiency or address consumer needs. And this wider vision also helps them think outside the boundaries of their company and imagine different ways in which their industry's eco-system might be configured. Such collaboration and communication across multiple disciplines and companies also spurs innovation. We believe this business-led innovation is the fastest way to create more sustainable societies and move our society back from the brink. Once responsible or sustainable innovation becomes a key factor in product and service development, the business world will lead us to a more sustainable future.

In summary, the social, spiritual and environmental consciousness that is gradually spreading through our society is a natural and necessary response to the excessive materialism and capitalism of recent decades. Like a body protecting itself against excess, we are evolving to a new way of thinking. This new perspective rejects both the selfishness of mindless consumerism and the selfishness of businesses for their narrow focus on short-term financial gain. The aim is to achieve a more responsible, connected and conscious economic and social life. We are hopefully heading towards a new paradigm that is essentially a transition from the "ego-system" to the "eco-system."

Towards a new paradigm

Everything we have presented in the previous sections indicates an urgent need for a different future –a place where humanity feels a sense of belonging to one global eco-system in which we all share equal responsibility. Currently, we are experiencing the transition to this new place: it is the turn of an era, controlled by a different way of thinking, a new paradigm.

For the organizational world especially, the journey to the new paradigm will be challenging. It involves 'unlearning' old, ingrained habits, and as any ex-smoker will tell you, that is never easy. It also implies learning new habits –showing meaningful consideration for the staff as real people, for the society in which they operate, and for the sustainability of the planet's resources which they must respect. It means the real development of a mission that benefits not only investors but also the eco-system to which they belong as a whole. As Michael Porter and Mark Kramer say in their article "*Creating Shared Value*" [13], businesses must reconnect company success with social progress. There are a number of initiatives to help them.

The United Nations proposed to measure organizations not only by their economic results but also by their social and environmental ones, adopting this new vision in their Millennium resolutions in 2000. This introduced the business world to the concept of reporting results against the three pillars of sustainability (economy, social, environment) or "triple bottom line" as it has become known. Gunter Pauli goes a step further in his latest book, "The Blue Economy" proposing companies to move from 'triple bottom line' perspectives to quadruple cash flows. Based on the inter-connected way nature itself works, he proposes a new type of business design in which the manufacturing waste from one product is explicitly designed to become the raw material for another, helping sustainability in addition to making a new cash flow. For example, leftovers mixed with dirty water can generate energy, bio-gas and fertilizer as well as making money. These and other initiatives have been tried out with some success.

The Global Reporting Initiative (GRI) is a non-profit organization promoting sustainability through the publication of a standard framework and guidelines for the production of sustainability reports, establishing the principles and indicators that organizations can use to measure and publicize their economic, environmental and social performance. It is being used worldwide.

These are encouraging early signs of businesses beginning to respond to the challenge of transformation. However, there are still many people and businesses anchored in the selfish paradigm of the last century, in which everything revolves around the promotion of mindless consumption in order to meet the expectations of investors for the next financial quarter. Let us look into some examples of what we call old paradigm thinking, which still prevails unfortunately, although not across all organizations.

One example is how we are asked to adapt to the job description rather than the other way round. In the new paradigm, organizations that show respect for the individuals in all the physical, emotional and spiritual dimensions of their personality will be more able to attract and keep talent around their business model. Many young people report that they want jobs where they feel fully respected and recognized, a trend that will no doubt increase in the future. But many people still suffer in organizations or workplaces where they are not allowed to be themselves or, worse still, are asked to do things that conflict with their values.

Another stubborn example of the old paradigm is the search for competitive advantage through reducing manufacturing costs without showing any consideration for where or how this is done. Jobs moved offshore devastate the communities left behind. And moving jobs or sources offshore to lower cost solutions is done without promoting fair business or developing projects that generate progress and wealth in the lower cost locations, including the poorest strata in society.

The old model is also the paradigm of "command-and-control" structures built along the lines of armies and warfare; indeed much of the language of old paradigm uses war terminology (launching products, price wars, sales force or divisions). This is a world of rigid uniformity, simple obedience and the mentality that everybody outside the organization is the enemy —competitors and suppliers are to be beaten down. It is not a world that prizes diversity of opinion and collaborative efforts. There is little space for emotions, intuition, love or spirituality —the very qualities that make us human.

E.F. Schumacher published his essay "*Buddhist Economics*" in 1966 [14]. It is one of the hundred most influential books written since the Second World War, according to the *London Times*. It spoke even then about sustainable economies. Schumacher makes a distinction between what he called the "modern economy", referring to the capitalist developed economy in the Western world (the old paradigm in our language), and what he calls "Buddhist Economics" which, devoid of any religious connotations, is very much in line with what this book calls new paradigm economics. The so called "modern economy", still prevalent nowadays, believes that the key measure of success is the total amount of material goods produced in a specific period. This paradigm considers that material goods are more important than people, and that consumption is more important than creativity. The standard of living is measured by annual consumption, assuming that those who consume the most somehow "are better" than those who consume less.

New paradigm economics also seeks to increase individual well-being, but with a minimum consumption of resources. So success will not be measured by production, sales or goods consumption but through the creation of meaningful employment for all those who want it. While the old paradigm aims simply to increase consumption, the "new paradigm" tries to find the optimum level of consumption, not the maximum. Countries which base the success of their economies on a heavy consumption of goods, such as the U.S. or most of Europe, will need much more effort and determination to change than other countries in Africa or Asia (such as Burma) where consumption does not have the same importance. For example, Bhutan, a small country situated in the Himalayas, is officially designated an underdeveloped country. But it chooses to rely on an indicator of Gross National Happiness (GNH) instead of the Gross Domestic Product (GDP) to measure the development of its country. Inspired by this example, many countries and supranational organizations have already made the effort to develop similar indicators, different from the traditional ones. This is, doubtless, a vision of the new paradigm.

Schumacher also drew attention to the irreconcilable tension between business executives and employees in the old paradigm. On the one hand, the owners treat human resources merely as an "input"; a cost to be reduced as much as possible or even eliminated through automation. On the other hand, the employee regards work as a personal sacrifice, giving up personal comfort in exchange for a salary. From this point of view, the ideal thing is to earn a living with the minimum effort or, if possible, by not even working at all. In this old paradigm, the ideals of both sides are hard to reconcile: right wing politics favors the business executive as the job creator, whereas left wing politics favors the innocent and exploited worker. The view of the new paradigm is very similar to Schumacher's Buddhist Economics, which sees the essence of civilization not as material gain but as purification of the human character. In his view, work has three purposes: to develop individual faculties, to reduce egocentrism through teamwork in working towards a common goal and to produce products and services needed for a "holy life" –again, this phrase is devoid of religious connotations and speaks of the spiritual dimensions of work.

Because work is more than simply earning a living; it is a way of expressing dignity in life. In 1982 in Olot, Catalonia (Spain), *La Fageda* was created. This is a business project which gives work to a group that has always been marginalized in society: the mentally ill and mentally handicapped. Its founder Cristobal Colón wanted to set up an organization offering dignified and financially sustainable workplaces for these people. Nowadays, *La Fageda* is a benchmark of the success in the new paradigm and of social entrepreneurship.

The nature of the work in the new paradigm assumes that workers want to do their best as it is an opportunity for individual development and realization. Thus, the business executive will look for ways of organizing the work so that individuals will perform to the best of their ability in a workplace where trust, delegation of duties and responsibility are the main components. Trust must be earned and for leaders to be trusted they must first trust others [15]. In the paradigm of the last century, however, work was based on a lack of trust with the employees looking for ways of "shirking" their responsibilities, and the business executive therefore looking for ways of tightly controlling and measuring individual and group performance.

The old paradigm also believes that the figure of the "self" is an entity separate from the rest of the world. This egocentric view is responsible for the misuse of limited natural resources such as water, coal and oil trees, to name a few. The point of reference used in the old paradigm regarding the different sources of energy available such as coal, petrol, wood or wind energy is unit cost. The cheapest is considered the best, so doing it, would be regarded as "non-economic" (according to this paradigm). The new paradigm defends another approach: Non-renewable energy should only be used in cases of necessity and the use of renewable energy should be prioritized at all times.

Given that the planet's resources in non-renewable energy are scarce and not uniformly distributed, it is obvious that ever increasing levels of exploitation will inevitably produce violence among human beings, desperate to secure access to a dwindling resource. Therefore, self-sufficient communities will be less likely to get involved in violent acts compared to those whose very existence depends on international exchange mechanisms such as petrol. Supplying local needs with local resources is the most reasonable way of establishing sustainable economic life.

Meeting human needs from sources far afield is regarded as a triumph in the old paradigm −an example of the ability of capitalism to shrink the planet through impressive feats of logistics. Consider the delocalization trend, pervasive in recent years; eating strawberries at Christmas shows a lack of respect for the planet if these strawberries were produced in countries in the other hemisphere and transported by air, consequently causing an unnecessary emission of CO_2.

Like Schumacher's Buddhist Economics, the new business paradigm integrates and balances material well-being with spiritual health. We are not referring to any particular religion –each religion has its own interpretation of spirituality, but to an essential and universal spirituality, an undeniable part of every human being, something that cannot be renounced. We defend that the integration of spiritual values in our economic progress could be done without producing any conflicts. Could anyone argue that the old paradigm, practiced without much consideration for spiritual values, has produced satisfactory results in the past few years? Exorbitant unemployment rates, the collapse of the rural economy, a rapid deterioration of the planet and a growth in the urban proletariat devoid of spiritual nourishment.

Acceptance of the new paradigm is doubtlessly a difficult change not only at a social and business level but obviously also at a personal level. This book is not a self-help book for the individual but a tool to help organizations (public and private) to make a gradual transition to the new paradigm. However, as far as possible, it does intend to inspire organizational leaders at an individual level for everyone's benefit. In fact, with this book we propose that the leaders go back to their origins, to simplicity, to rational use, to common sense and human values. And then use their leadership qualities to move their organizations forward through the change that is upon us.

Evidence of change

Organizations facing external changes respond in a similar psychological way to individuals. First, we have to face the shock that something is no longer the same. Something in our environment has indeed changed. When the change is large, it can take people some time simply to overcome the shock to the system – it can produce numbness, a stupor that makes adjustment difficult. Once we have overcome our initial shock, we will have to "digest" the change so we can begin to gradually accept what this new situation means for us. In the second stage, we observe our environment very carefully and ask some questions to verify the authenticity of what we can see and what is happening to us. In this stage, it is very useful to have lots of signals, steady evidence that validates real change has happened. These signals are crucial to completing our internalization of change so we can move on to third and final stage: taking action.

In a similar way, if we are exposed to a multitude of acts, situations and information of all types that are evidence that the new paradigm has begun for most of the planet's population, then perhaps it will be easier for us to accept the irrevocable change of an era. And this will release us so we can take positive action and make our contribution, whether individually, from our position in an organization or better still, both.

We will therefore go on to list some more of these perhaps small signs that the new paradigm thinking is already here with us.

The first example is to be found in all the demonstrations and popular occupation movements that took place in public places in 2011, a year of protest. Starting with the "The Arab Spring" that began in January and spread across many countries, it was followed in the developed world by the 15-M Movement (or the Outraged movement) that began in Spain in May. Within a short time, this citizen movement spread worldwide. September brought a Wall Street Movement as well as other demonstrations around the globe: Moscow, Great Britain, Germany, Israel, Switzerland, Nigeria and Mongolia, all tapping into unease with the current economic and social systems.

We have also seen how the "financial crisis", which has been spreading through the globalized world since 2008 (and which was still hitting some countries in southern Europe in 2013), is no longer viewed simply as an economic crisis; it has become a crisis of values.

According to an opinion poll carried out in Germany and Austria, almost 90% of the population wants an "alternative economic order". In 2008 Christian Felber had begun to develop the basis for such an alternative in his Common Welfare Economy, described in his book "New Values for the Economy [16]. An alternative to consumerism and capitalism". The "Common Welfare Economy" tries to establish a legally binding framework in which values orientated towards the common good can prosper. In response to this publication, numerous business executives have got together to discuss and further develop his model.

We can also see signs of change in governments. In 2011 the Catalan Government (Generalitat de Catalunya), already concerned about the promotion of specific values in our society, launched a pioneering initiative to develop a national plan to promote Values.

In the educational system we have also seen some evidence, (it must be said limited at present) of the adoption of more systemic education in accordance with our current global reality.

Banks do not want to seem out of step either and "sustainable banking" has existed for years. These are banks which invest all their capital in projects of social and environmental interest instead of seeking to enrich their investors. Currently, this is the only kind of banking that in fact is growing significantly.

Previously, we mentioned the increasing importance of the Corporate Social Responsibility in private companies. More and more companies who had resisted or ignored these concepts are now taking a 180 degree turn –perhaps motivated by current successful social and environmental programs from their competitors and in other industries [17].

Another very relevant example is the existence, literally speaking, of millions of NGOs all over the world, dedicated to humanity and ecology. There are a growing number of 'conscious' people who, unable to find a meaning in daily corporate life, prefer to dedicate themselves to work that has a higher purpose for them – whether humanistic or environmental.

There is also an increasingly long list of thought leaders focusing on these issues and raising awareness around the world. A remarkable example is Muhammad Yunus, who developed the concept of micro credit. Micro credits are small loans given to poorer people unable to qualify for a traditional bank loan. Yunus was awarded the Nobel Peace Prize in 2006 for his efforts to encourage social and economic development at the bottom strata of society.

In line with the aforementioned, there are a growing number of successful national and international conferences and forums (some on-line) which bring together multidisciplinary groups in order to debate and explore solutions to the global challenges that we are facing nowadays. The success of the TED initiative (*"Ideas Worth Spreading"*), is just one example of this phenomena but there are a growing number of still smaller initiatives worth noting like Conscious Leadership Connection [18], Conscious Capitalism [19] and Wholehearted Leadership [20], among others.

Similarly, a large number of people also meet regularly in think-tanks with the aim of helping the community and improving "the system." We, ourselves, for example, have already taken part in three of these: one in Sweden (*The Medinge Group*), focusing on Conscious Branding, another in Holland, (*De Baak Think Tank*), focusing on Post-Crisis Leadership, and the other of our own creation in Barcelona (*Pinea3's Feel-Tank*), focusing on Conscious Leadership and Organizational Prosperity.

There is also a growing number of training, educational and consulting organizations specifically focusing on the new paradigm and the need to prepare individuals and organizations. Their methodologies and practices all deal with the most human aspects of leadership and aim to raise business leaders' self-awareness and consciousness so they can meet the new challenges of the era. A prominent example is The Center for Creative Leadership, an organization that since 1970 is committed to advancing the understanding and practice of leadership for the benefit of individuals, organizations and society at large.

The quantity of videos, articles and books (like this one) that transmit the same fundamental messages, makes it difficult to reference them all. And we should not overlook the worldwide explosion of publications about personal growth and self-help in the last twenty years, which clearly shows that people are beginning to look for new ways of leading their lives —more conscious ways of co-existing with others and with the environment, and for the answers internally Watch the movie-documentary "I AM, The shift is about to hit the fan" [21] if you have not yet seen it, another good example of the many people that after realizing that there is a better way, is promoting reflection on the subject.

Staying at the personal level, we can see other signs of unease with our rampant consumerism in the movement to healthier eating. This has already led to a shift to more natural, unprocessed products. And people in the Western World are increasingly looking for alternatives to traditional medicine that focuses on reducing the symptoms of illnesses, not necessarily their causes. We refer here to homeopathy, chiropractics, as well as several ancient Eastern practices which are penetrating the Western consciousness powerfully: acupuncture, Ayurveda and several kinds of energy healing. And alongside this interest in Eastern healing wisdom, there has been a considerable increase in global yoga practices in recent years. It is estimated that more than 400 million people are practicing this ancient technique to unite the body, soul and mind. The number of people practicing meditation is also growing in the world. Sindya N. Bhanoo, for example, expressed her surprise in an article in The *New York Times* [22], at the large number of people who were meditating in the San Francisco bay area and an increasing number of centers dedicated to some kind of meditation training.

Researchers are also interested in meditation and mindfulness practices, especially to understand how does is help employee satisfaction and wellbeing as well as organizational effectiveness. A few but relevant studies exist already that show that meditative practices can help reduce stress, increase concentration, develop empathy, improve decision making and enhance self-awareness, among other positive effects [23].

As it may be expected, the media is responding to these higher levels of interest. Many television, magazine and radio programs today are addressing and popularizing concepts such as emotional intelligence, the energetic nature of things and meditation practices. These ideas are now moving into the mainstream.

In the employment world, another trend is the increasing number of people who are leaving successful jobs (according to old paradigm standards) in order to devote themselves to helping others through coaching, for example, seeking a better work-life balance while trying to find more fulfillment and meaning in their working hours.

It is obvious that this list of observations and situations is not acceptable (or intended) as any kind of rigorous mathematical proof of a change of era. However, it gives an impressionistic sense of the scale of changes that are taking place. These often occur at an individual level and are therefore rarely fully appreciated until we look at all the elements together. The observations mentioned above will help us get started with the second stage of our personal and organizational process of change.

We all have access to this information, but only if we want to see it. In this book, we encourage all the people who acknowledge this new view of the world to add their weight to the critical mass needed to produce change globally. There is no need to force those who cannot see or do not want to see it. If enough conscious leaders step forward, a whole organization and eventually a whole society will "wake up". In this way, we can start to change our daily reality from the old to the new paradigm. The rest of this book shows how to lead within your organization on this important mission.

PART II

THE META-MODEL
OF CONSCIOUS LEADERSHIP

- From Concept to Practice
- Everything is Energy
- A Systemic View
- An Integral Vision of Existence
- Living Organizations
- Conscious Leadership
- Organizational Prosperity

From concept to practice

In the first part of the book we described the present reality as we see it, defining the context in which we are now living. We concluded that there is a new paradigm of thought; a paradigm we will all have to come to terms with, in one way or another. In this second part of the book, we will try to define this new paradigm in more detail, using a model that facilitates its understanding. We call it the 'Meta-Model of Conscious Leadership'.

The Meta-Model rests on three 'universal concepts' that are shared by most people today: Everything is Energy, A Systemic View and an Integral Vision of Existence. These are described separately below. In the next level, the Meta–Model takes a higher level of concretion, when the three 'universal concepts' are applied to the world of organizations through three 'basic principles': Living Organizations, Conscious Leadership and Organizational Prosperity. The last piece of the model introduces a 'transformational methodology' with a highly practical application: Organizational Healing, which is the main objective of this book.

The Meta–Model therefore is a road map to guide us from conceptual knowledge to a transformational methodology that heals organizations. Building healthier and more prosperous organizations is indeed the main objective of this book.

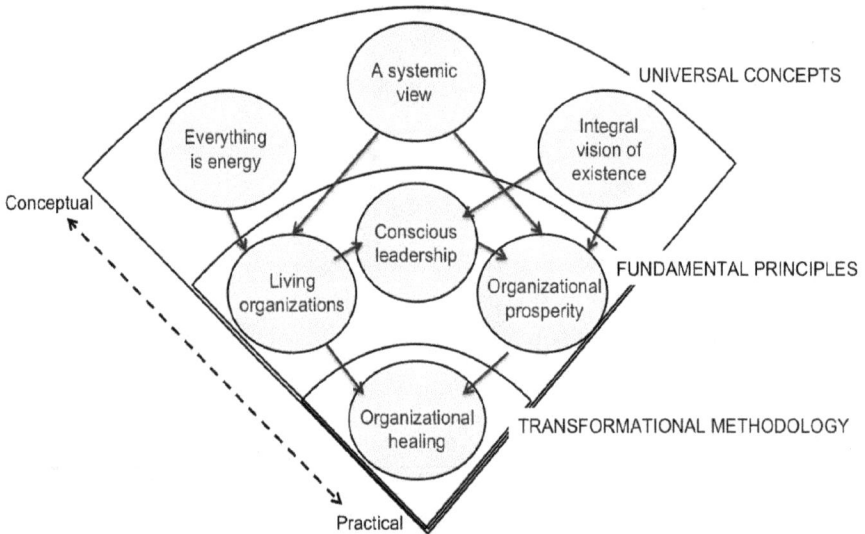

As can be seen in the diagram above, the Meta–Model is a 'piece of cake', where the 'whole cake' might represent *all* the possible views and descriptions of the new paradigm. This 'slice' is our particular approach, which we modestly want to share with the world. Let us look at the model in some more detail.

The three 'Universal Concepts' –the starting points for the model are different elements of the new paradigm and are therefore closely interrelated. The three concepts are widely shared by opinion leaders, scientists, authors, consultants, entrepreneurs, executives and conscious individuals around the world. To show their most universal nature, these 'Universal Concepts' are placed on the outer perimeter of the Meta–Model. In the next smaller section are the three 'Basic Principles' that are used as a platform to build our transformational work with organizations. And the point of the 'piece of cake' is where all the previous concepts and principles of the Meta-Model are combined in a radical methodology to improve organizational health and prosperity.

Each of these seven elements (ellipses in the diagram) operate separately but are related to each other in subtle and nuanced ways. The most significant relationships are marked with arrows in the model above. If we are truly interested in helping our organizations perform better, if we really want to develop our company and its workers, if we are striving for effective team work; in short, if we want to reach the full potential of our organization, then we have to get these seven elements to work for us in a practical and integrated way. That is the purpose of the Meta-Model of Conscious Leadership; a model that we think can finally bring the new world paradigm into corporate consciousness.

In our experience, people who understand and share the ideas behind the model can begin to 'connect' in a special way. Even if they begin as strangers, they quickly establish deep relationships and begin to vibrate at the same frequency. A common energy is generated, connecting and bringing them together to undertake joint actions and initiatives. And the initiatives truly improve the health of the organization, free of the old toxins of cynicism, office politics and narrow self-interest that are endemic in organizational bodies today.

We will now look at each of the elements described in the Meta-Model in detail, from the most conceptual to the most practical.

Everything is energy

Every age, generation and culture has its own assumptions: 'the earth is flat', 'matter is composed of atoms with their nuclei and electrons', or 'one race is superior to another'. But what assumptions can stand the test of time? What are the big assumptions of our era? In our search for reality, Science embraces the fundamental willingness to discard accepted or long-held positions if our search finds that the truth is different. Surprisingly (or not) Buddhism shares the exact same attitude [2]. A small seed of doubt in our starting assumptions can help us widen our field of perception and open up the possibility of embracing a larger system of beliefs.

Physics is one of the essential disciplines of human knowledge. It has evolved dramatically in recent years. The scientific discoveries provided by quantum physics in particular offer an impressive view of the world, more integrative and comprehensive than our previous understanding. Quantum physics shows us that everything is energy and possibilities, and proves that the old mechanistic view of reality cannot explain many of the phenomena we observe today.

Until recently, subatomic physics, focusing on the micro-cosmos, and macro-cosmos physics walked separately. Quantum physics attempts to integrate both research fields and suggests matter is no longer what we traditionally thought it was: something static and predictable. In the words of Deepak Chopra, "the raw material of the universe is nonmaterial" or as Janna Levin states that "the fabric of the universe is just a coherent weave from the same threads that make our bodies [24].

But do we really know what it means when we say that everything is energy and possibilities? In quantum physics laboratories, molecules apparently come and go, but where to? Scientists say it is as if parallel universes existed simultaneously. This phenomenon is known as 'quantum superposition', which means that a particle can be in many places at the same time. It is one of the most unique features of the quantum world; that the materialization of energy has many possibilities until a specific form is chosen. Heisenberg, quantum physics pioneer, had already declared that atoms were not things but just trends. Quantum physics only calculates possibilities, so the question is: who or what chooses among the multiple possibilities for the event of experience to take place? No one knows for sure who chooses, but we do know that our intention, our state of consciousness, has a decisive influence on the experience observed.

Let us see what this means at a subatomic level. Scientists have proven with several laboratory studies, even with highly precise photographic instruments, that molecules change their behavior depending on whether or not they are being observed. When they are not, they behave as a wave of infinite possibilities, but when observed, they appear as particles placed in a certain position [25]. The observer changes the experience! Scientists know what effect the "observer" has from the quantum physics point of view, but they cannot exactly define who or what it is. They have searched the brain but nothing with the form of the observer has been found. Some say it is like the 'soul of the machine', our consciousness. According to Dalai Lama, this paradox (the wave-particle duality) seems to suggest that, unless we accord some kind of intelligence to electrons, at the subatomic level two of the most important principles of logic, the law of contradiction and the law of the excluded middle, appear to break down [2].

If we believe there is only one specific reality, we cannot move forward. But if reality means possibilities, we might wonder: How can I change reality and how can I improve it? According to the old way of thinking, there is little we can do to change things because the objects are already there, guided by deterministic laws. According to the new view, however, everything is energy in the form of possibilities and we choose indeed the real experience we will have in our consciousness. Therefore, we create our own reality. Dr. Amit Goswami views the world as possible timelines of reality, until we choose. Then energy is embodied in a given reality.

At this point, you might be thinking: this is all well and good at a subatomic level, but what does it mean for the reality we see and touch every day? The work of Dr. Masaru Emoto, author of the international bestseller "Messages from Water" [26] approaches this answer. Emoto shows how the molecular structure of water, the most receptive of the four elements, surprisingly reacts to non-physical events. His experiments show that using mental stimuli on water triggers significant differences between molecules. For example, glass bottles of distilled water left overnight with labels expressing different feelings and intentions ("love" vs. "hate", for instance). Very different molecular structures were observed the day after. Similar changes were recorded in the molecular state of water before and after a Buddhist monk had blessed it. As with quantum physics, Emoto concludes that thought or intention are the 'alma mater' of everything. And if an intention written on a label has this effect on water, what might be the effect of all our thoughts, positive and negative, on our body, (which after all is mostly composed of water)? Or the collective effect of the thoughts of our teams on the company? And the effect of all these thoughts or energy flows on organizations? And on the whole world?

We now know our consciousness has an impact on the real world. What we think changes the world, and we do not mean bending spoons or making rocks levitate. These changes are much more subtle. For instance, since the 60s, experiments have been conducted with random number generators, where participants are asked to try to produce more 1s than 0s. Over the years and after many experiments, it has been proven that the intention of a person affects the result of the random machine [25].

We will now look at another equally striking example of this reality. In 1993 in Washington, a global crime capital at the time, four thousand volunteers were doing long meditation sessions for a full day with the intention to reduce crime in the city by 25%. The head of police in Washington had said that it would have to snow one meter for crime to be reduced by that much but the FBI later confirmed that crime rates had indeed fallen by 25% during the experiment.

Another example of the effect of our thoughts on reality is a study conducted among 40 women suffering from breast cancer. The doctor told them all that the chemotherapy would make them lose their hair. Only 20 were treated with chemotherapy. The other twenty were just made to believe so, but 60% of the latter group lost their hair as if they had also been treated [27]. Scientists, though, also say that most people do not alter reality in a consistent and substantial way because they do not think they are able to.

As surprising as these scientific findings might sound, they are actually common sense. The fact that a positive person attracts positivity in his accomplishments is something we have always known from intuition or experience. Many ancient spiritual beliefs also claimed it to be this way long ago. Today, some scientists have approached Buddhist monks to tell them they have now proved at prestigious US universities what monks have been saying for thousands of years [2]. In his book "The Universe in a Single Atom", Dalai Lama refers to the parallels that have been drawn between Nagarjuna's Buddhist philosophy of emptiness and quantum phisics.

David Albert, Amit Goswami, William Tiller, Fred Alan Wolf and John Hagelin, some of the most prestigious scientists from renowned universities like Columbia, Oregon, Stanford and UCLA (among others) produced a documentary film 'What the bleep do we know!?' [28] that has been seen all over the world. The film explores the connections between quantum physics, neurobiology, human consciousness and everyday reality. After the first film's success, they developed "What the bleep!? Down the rabbit hole?" [25] and in 2010 they released a third film: "What now!?", a six-hour documentary to satisfy those willing to know more about this topic. We recommend them. They are a great way to start opening your mind to the new reality we discuss in this chapter.

In the second film scientists discuss what they call one of the weirdest things in quantum physics: "entanglement", which deconstructs the concept of space as we know it. When two electrons are formed together, what we do to one of them appears to instantly affect the other, even when they are miles apart. It seems that despite the distance, the particles are still connected in some way. Since everything was 'interwoven' at the time of the Big Bang, everything is still in motion, which means that the construction of space is an illusion and that everything (and therefore everyone) is connected in some way. Through this glimpse of light we can certainly approach the concept of a single consciousness. Understanding 'we are all one' indeed is a breath of fresh air that helps position ourselves in a new paradigm. On the other side, seeing things inherently divided and disconnected has lead in the past to various ideologies that tend to divide humanity such as racisms and extreme nationalisms.

Becoming aware that each of us as individuals, members of a team or an organization, or as part of society, are energy systems with infinite possibilities should be food for thought for all management thinkers. In their article "Team Energy" [29] Cos and Tarré propose a model for energy management in teams. Their premise is that depending on how organizations think and the attitude of management teams, a specific organizational 'energy field' is created that inevitably conditions the organization's results and performance.

This chapter is not intended to describe quantum physics, how to manage the springs of the universe or who 'the observer' is. However, like millions of people around the world, we are becoming more and more comfortable with this new way of viewing the universe and therefore living life more consciously. We believe it will bring about more satisfaction, better results and certainly a higher level of happiness. Thus, becoming aware that "everything is energy and possibilities" is a cornerstone of this new paradigm and the Meta-Model of Conscious Leadership.

A Systemic View

Let us explore the second 'universal concept' in the Meta-Model of Conscious Leadership: A Systemic View of the universe and all its life forms. This concept is closely related to the concepts we have seen in the previous section: Everything is Energy, since the basis for systemic understanding is the energetic understanding.

Each element of a system has a specific function. Could we drive a car if every part of the vehicle did not fulfill its function in the system?

Imagine the wheels occupying the space of the engine, or a battery in the place of the steering wheel. It is easy to see that a car is a system from a mechanical point of view, but as we have seen in the previous chapter, 'reality' goes beyond what we can see with our eyes. The mechanistic view defines the system as a set of rules and principles rationally intertwined. But this definition is not enough to explain how our environment works. It is therefore essential that we look at some bases of systemic thinking in this chapter.

Since the General Systems Theory was first proposed by Ludwig von Bertanlanffy in 1937, it has developed over the 20th century through most disciplines: psychiatry, physiology, engineering, biology, psychology, physics and anthropology, creating a large body of specialized literature and great works we cannot discuss adequately in this section. However, we will pay special attention to developments in recent years, when the systemic approach aims at understanding a global hyper-linked world. We will mainly focus on the work with organizations and teams in line with the objectives of this book.

Peter Senge was the main reference of organizational development in the 90s and he popularized the notion of organizations as systems in his seminal book "The Fifth Discipline" [30]. Organizational development has advanced by leaps and bounds since the new systemic knowledge was incorporated into efforts aimed at helping improve organizations and their teams. There are many new practical tools and implementation methods currently taught in the most innovative development programs. When working with natural teams, for example, 'systemic coaching' has recently gained great importance.

Most intervention methods focus on organizations' and teams' behavioral patterns and help them acquire the skills and tools to explore, clarify and then free themselves from these patterns. This allows them to expand to higher relationship levels. Kelly Simmons and David Hudnut apply six factors, characteristic of human systems, to improve team performance: Structure, Homeostasis, Relationship, Mind Maps, Free Will, and Chaos [31].

The key feature of systemic methods is analyzing human behavior not as an isolated entity, but as part of a whole system with all its key relationships and processes. In 1988, Arnold Mindell gave birth to the concept of "deep democracy" [32] to describe the importance of being aware of and appreciating the different levels of experience in a phenomenon. This type of work, known as "process work", integrates concepts of physics, psychology, anthropology and spirituality, and is already being success-fully applied in many areas of life, organizations and societies. American politicians have begun to use these techniques to better understand the systemic relationship between the ruling party and the opposition.

Another example of the systemic development in recent years is the work of German philosopher and psychotherapist Bert Hellinger, who pioneered a revolutionary technique to reveal the hidden dynamics in any system. Hellinger uses what is known as 'constellations' or 'systemic configurations'. They were first applied for therapeutic uses in family systems but quickly spread to the field of health and education.

Gunthard Weber, together with his colleagues Jan Jacob Stam and Mathias Varga, have taken Hellinger's pioneering ideas further and incor-porated them in the professional and organizational environment. This is a very recent development that has spanned over the last fifteen years, laying the foundations for what we could call 'quantum skills' in the con-sulting practice of the 21st century.

In his book "*Fields of Connection: The Practice of Organisational Constel-lations*" [33] Stam claims it is easy to forget that we are part of a larger whole in our daily lives; lives so full of challenges and personal limita-tions. The "systemic" perspective of the world helps us become aware of the many counter-productive mechanisms and dynamics in systems that we do not normally perceive. These dynamics might, at any one point, paralyze us and prevent us from acting to our full potential.

Constellation work at an organizational level, for example, can bring light to any fundamental truth of the system, beyond the personal opin-ions, prejudices and snap judgments that so often filter and distort the truth. Such work can help us gain better awareness, give us new ideas about the performance of organizational systems and show how the peo-ple working in them can fully develop their potential.

In Part III of the book, under the description of the seventh chakra, we will provide more concrete examples about the meaning an implica-tions of a systemic understanding for the well-functioning of organiza-tions that will bring down to earth this important concept.

The real power of the new paradigm becomes evident in this more advanced area of systemic development. Here the systemic and the en-ergetic understanding are intertwined in surprising ways to offer a new vision of the world, both more complete and more integrated.

Knowing that everything is related in the universe, that we are all interconnected and we are all linked to the universe in its most basic level might be a good approach to understand what spirituality is from a systemic perspective. Albert Einstein is claimed to have said that a human being is part of a whole we call universe, a part limited in time and space that experiences itself, its thoughts and feelings, as something separated from the rest, a kind of delusion of its consciousness.

In short, we will better understand reality if we regard ourselves and our surroundings (our team, organizations, society or our planet) as a set of closely interrelated systems. Through this higher consciousness we can then see and connect with all the possibilities these systems can offer. A better systemic understanding will definitely bring us many opportunities to improve our lives, the health of our organizations and therefore everyone's prosperity.

An Integral Vision of Existence

The third 'universal concept' in the Meta-Model refers to the Integral Vision of Existence. We are much more than a physical body or a brain with legs. Human beings have four dimensions: physical, emotional, mental and spiritual, though we often neglect some of them. This chapter is closely related to the previous two chapters because we are made of energy, in its many forms, and we are also a system, a living system. We are part of a whole and we are interconnected to it.

"*Gnóthi seautón*" ('Know Thyself') read the Greek inscription in the *pronaos* of the temple of Apollo at Delphi over 3000 years ago. The wise men of ancient Greece had already come to the conclusion that self-knowledge was the key starting point for understanding our lives and the world around us. We need to develop a complete vision of the human being, not only from knowing our physical and intellectual abilities, but also from understanding our emotions and the spiritual being in all of us. We can only reach a deeper level of self-awareness through working towards an integral vision of human life. Ken Wilber, one of the most recognized contemporary philosophers states that an Integral Vision of existence ensures that we are utilizing the full range of resources for the situation, leading to a greater likelihood of success and fulfillment [34].

A look to our inner self is the key to solving the problems we face in life, both individually or collectively. The deep crisis affecting the whole of society and each of us all directly somehow, has its origin in a lack of self-knowledge.

There is no doubt that progress in human knowledge throughout the 20th century has been impressive in all fields of science. However, something in our social pattern has led us to the extreme degeneration of coexistence. At some point we lost our way; we forgot that we are human beings who need to be realized fully in all human dimensions. We must reconnect with our integral self if we are to lay the foundations of the new paradigm. It is through this comprehensive view of the human being that we will realize we live in a world full of energy and possibilities where everything is perfectly interrelated in a great system. As we saw in the section stating everything is energy, the reality we create depends on our personal and collective consciousness. This integral vision of existence had never been more necessary for individuals, communities and organizations of all types. This is one of the critical implications of the new paradigm for companies: seeing workers as human beings with four dimensions –the mental, emotional, spiritual and, of course, the physical component.

The Mental Component

The intellectual level is where we spend most of our time, planning or fretting about the future and remembering the past. Our intellectual capacity has developed considerably, but the thinking mind (cognitive) is just one of the functions of our brain. In recent years, neuroscience has made great progress through the development of scanners and other devices that measure brain activity, which has helped us better understand the most complex of all our organs. In his book "Evolve Your Brain" [35], Joe Dispenza explains that although the brain processes about 400,000 million bits of information per second, we are only aware of about 2,000. Most of our brain activity goes unnoticed by us – that is, it does not enter our consciousness. This is intuitively obvious from a simple and common example. We are capable of sitting in poor posture for hours on end, unable to perceive the messages our body is sending until it sends us a sharp pain that we cannot ignore. However, through meditation or other techniques we can train our minds and and eventually perceive some of the 99.5% of information that goes unnoticed. The new paradigm calls for a more integrated human being who strives to reach his full potential in a balanced way.

The Emotional Component

In 1995, after decades where only the rational mind seemed to be important in business literature, Daniel Goleman released his famous book on "Emotional Intelligence" [36]. Emotional intelligence is both the ability to recognize our own feelings (and those of others) and the ability to manage them. Goleman believes that emotional intelligence can be organized around five skills: knowing our own emotions and feelings, recognizing them, managing them, creating our own motivation, and managing relationships. His re-emphasis on the 're-discovery' of our emotions and the acceptance of them in our organizational life was certainly a breakthrough on the road to the new paradigm.

Emotions are designed to chemically reinforce some elements in the long-term memory and for that our body uses some of the most sophisticated chemistry in the known universe. There are specific chemicals for anger, for sadness, for self-pity —indeed, there is a chemical for each emotional state we experience. When these substances are produced too frequently, our body enters a state of 'cold turkey'; a compelling need for that emotion to be created, even when it is clearly harmful to us. Emotions themselves are not bad, the risk is creating a biochemical addiction to them. Heroin works by using exactly the same receptor mechanisms on cells as our emotional chemicals. It is easy to understand that if we can get hooked on heroin, we can get hooked on specific emotions. If you cannot control your emotional state, you are addicted to it and addictions are patterns that keep us tied to lower levels of consciousness.

Yet, there is hope: the latest advances in neuroscience show that change is possible even at an elderly age. Think of the influence our thoughts, intentions and awareness could have on ourselves and our environment. What we think and the emotions we feel are closely related. Seeing ourselves as integral beings and developing deeper self-knowledge can help us overcome the limitations that restrict our freedom as human beings and that dictate our behavior in social and organizational life.

The Spiritual Component

Spirituality is intrinsic to all of us and is often associated with religion. This is understandable, since for many years the realm of spirituality has been claimed by one religion or another. We are not talking about any individual religion or doctrine here, but about transcending them all and seeking the common connection. We then reach the innate spirituality of human beings as energy systems, which connects us to the universal energy system and also connects us to each other. In other words, spirituality means becoming aware that we are intrinsically energy; energy flowing and integrating with the rest of the cosmic energy. We do not deny any religious belief here. Indeed, one way or another, they all call us closer to the whole, to what each religion might call God and to a common consciousness. Awareness of this dimension of human existence is important for our health and personal integrity, especially in difficult times of global changes. Times like these.

Meditation is a proven technique for exploring and (re)integrating our spiritual dimension. It is not a subject commonly treated at an organizational level in Western societies. Yet it is slowly making its way into the business world, thanks to the most conscious and open-minded executives and to innovative organizations. For example, *Infojobs* Spain has already set up a meditation room where guided sessions are offered two days a week. In the East, such practices were incorporated in business long ago. As early as 1990 we could have lived the experience when working at *Omron Corporation* in Tokyo (Japan), where they already had relaxation-meditation rooms.

The Physical Component

We now enter the physical level, our material and tangible body. As this 'structure' is our house and shelter, we should keep it in the best possible condition. But we often neglect our body and take its functions for granted until it stops working one day. Or else in the best case, until it gives us a warning like the headache in the example we mentioned earlier. Awareness of bodily health has improved recently and more and more people are exercising regularly. We acknowledge that health care is good not only for your body, but also for your whole being. "*Mente, sana in corpore sano*". Several studies have shown that the most successful and top rank executives and leaders in companies are those with a better integrated physical activity.

We referred to meditation before; here we could talk about yoga. This ancient practice originating in India is not just physical exercise; it aims to integrate all the components of existence. In fact, the word *Yoga* means to unite, harmonize and integrate (body, mind and spirit). Fortunately, yoga practice is gaining popularity worldwide. Although the driver has largely been physical health and suppleness, we are hopeful that the original spirit of yoga will manifest itself too. There are now many initiatives to incorporate yoga in business as leaders look to improve the physical, mental and emotional development of their teams.

In summary then, we need to allow ourselves to connect with our most integral self and learn to be tuned to each of our four components in a more subtle way. When we do that, our self-confidence multiplies and our contribution to the system becomes increasingly significant. Balancing our physical, mental, emotional and spiritual self at all times is essential to a higher consciousness, one capable of supporting the new paradigm of the 21st century. This applies both to our personal lives and to the organizational level.

The best companies in the world are already attracting talent through programs that respond to this integral vision. An example is developing a plan for integral training and personal growth through volunteering. Tomorrow's leaders are unlikely to be those with an MBA from one of the world's most prestigious schools, but individuals who have developed and incorporated the four components in real life practice. Companies like *Ernst&Young* already have similar volunteer programs as part of talent development options.

Thus, *everything is energy, systemic view* and *integral vision of existence* are the three universal concepts that form the the philosophical base of the Meta-Model of Conscious Leadership. The next level of this model deals with making these three concepts more specific and meaningful to the world of organizations. Here we define the basic principles for improving organizations without overlooking the holistic view of the system. These principles are: 'living organizations', 'conscious leadership' and 'organizational prosperity', which we will discuss separately below.

Living Organizations

The first basic principle of the Meta-Model of Conscious Leadership is to consider that organizations are alive. When we ask individual entrepreneurs and managers if they think their organizations can be regarded as living organisms, almost everyone says yes, emphatically. Organizations are born; they grow, develop, have diseases, age, lose energy, and are eaten by other living organizations. Or they die because they have aged and have not been able to adapt to new realities. We can also say an organization is young and dynamic, or mature and rigid, that is a newborn (*start-up*), or that it is sick or dying and must be re-invented and transformed.

Arie de Geus wrote his bestseller 'The Living Company' [37] in 1997, after a successful career at Royal/Dutch Shell. Geus used the analogy of the living company to refer to those companies that can learn and adapt when faced with the cataclysm of sudden and dramatic change. The author posits a distinction between what he calls *financial* companies, only focused on producing wealth for a small group of individuals, and *living* companies, whose purpose is to fulfill their potential and endure as communities, evolving naturally as the world around them changes.

Only a year later, in 1998, Richard Barrett published *Liberating the Corporate Soul: Building a Visionary Organization* [38], which also highlights the importance of considering organizations as living entities rather than machines. Based on this metaphor, he builds an interesting model of organizational development. Unlike the more theoretical work of Geus, Barrett not only analyzes different companies to prove a common thread, but he develops a methodology for organizational change together with a number of transformation tools. Like Barret, we are also interested in providing a useful model for improving one of the core elements of an organization: its culture.

In 2000, William A. Guillory published *The Living Organization: Spirituality in the Workplace* [39], another book we think is ahead of its time. The author suggests that the organizations that will succeed in the 21st century are those led in a more humane way. These organizations deliberately choose a higher purpose to motivate and encourage employees; they strive to become places where everyone can do their job and find it meaningful. As John Renesch (the publisher) states in the preface, the book seeks to connect spirituality with successful companies.

In a more recent book on "Systemic Management" [40], Charles Fowler gives a different perspective of organizational management. In Fowler's systemic view, the company (for, or not-for profit) is compared to a living organism; to a system. A logical difference between classical management and systemic management is that while the former is based on personal creeds, beliefs and opinions, the second is more concerned with observable patterns.

Viewing organizations as living organisms offers a unique perspective to address problems differently than through old-school *management* styles. As Peter Senge says, most apparently successful large corporations, are simultaneously deeply sick [41]: they contain severe job stress and struggles over personal power and control. The general symptoms of the malaise are pervasive cynicism and resignation across the wider work force, resulting in a work environment that represses rather than triggers imagination, energy and personal commitment. The alternative to seeing profit-making companies as living organisms is seeing them as simply as money-making machines. And we all know what this has recently led to; dramatic financial crises and increasing wealth imbalances across the globe.

This correspondence between a living system like the human one and an organization can be understood from other perspectives as well. An example is the approach on systems consciousness by Ken Wilbert, author of the "*integral theory of consciousness*" [42]. Wilbert explains the concept of *holon*: a system contained in other systems. For instance, the cell is a lower *holon* forming organs, and these form bodies in a higher state or *holon*. In a similar way, individuals form teams and these form organizations that make up societies, which are higher levels of life and also have energy levels, the energy of the sum of its parts.

When you look at a company as a living organism, you start from the understanding that it creates its own processes, as if they were its cells, which in turn make up higher level systems. In any company, it is the people who allow work to be carried out, through their relational and communicative channels. Geus also claimed that companies die because their leaders and managers focus on the economic activity of goods and services production, and ignore that the essence or nature of any organization is to be a community of people [37].

Thanks to this organic approach we can review how we measure the welfare of our organizations. The concept of health makes sense if we talk about living organisms and move away from the mechanistic view that has prevailed for decades. In this old view, corporate health has been measured only by the amount of output (money) it generates for its owners. This may be a perfectly reasonable basis to judge a machine, but not a living system.

In his book *Leading Beyond The Walls* [43], Senge suggests that the vision of the organization as a living system requires critical changes in our business leadership. More conscious leaders are needed, with new principles and a new perspective. We need new definitions and new metaphors, that is, a new language. A daunting task, but if we think about it, none of this is truly new. The basis for understanding leadership in a world of

THE META-MODEL OF CONSCIOUS LEADERSHIP

living organizations existed before the rise of mechanistic thinking and, fortunately, has not been completely lost.

If organizations are living organisms, they will have a specific vital energy and should therefore respond to a given energy system. And this is the main contribution of this book, discussed in detail in Part III.

Conscious Leadership

In our view, there is a pressing need for organizations (and society in general) to be led by people with a higher level of consciousness. It is essential for the realization of the new paradigm. Therefore, we have included 'conscious leadership' as the second of the three 'basic principles' of the Meta-Model.

As we said in previous sections, a real, sustainable transformation to the new paradigm requires both a critical mass of people who feel this need and some sort of catalyst for this to take place.

More and more initiatives today are moving a surprisingly wide mass of the population towards more sensitive behaviors to the old paradigm. Social networks are increasingly contributing to this catalyst effect and there are many reasons why it is worth committing. An particular example is *Avaaz*, the largest Internet-based, international citizen movement in history. Avaaz.org promotes activism on issues like climate change, human rights and religious conflicts. Its main objective is to "ensure that the views and values of the peoples of the world influence decision-making" [44].

However, the Internet has an influence from the base, from the individual. While this is important and provides authenticity for change, it does not seem enough to mobilize the whole human kind in time. Let us remember that society and the planet have been signaling the problems for too long. We therefore need other stimuli to change the balance. We believe that there is a group with a greater strength and influence in society today: organizations (public and private), especially multinational companies and global corporations. Other people have seen this leverage point and are trying to influence such global leaders. We were happy to recently find that Weatherhead School of Management defend the same and explains it very clearly with the following three-step-logic: A) Companies have great, practical power in our society; B) Power equates responsibility; C) Responsibility means that this power should not be applied just to enrich the shareholders, but also make the world a somewhat better place.

Corporate leaders have great power of influence and many ordinary people (young and not so young) identify with them, certainly more readily than with politicians. Society, companies, individuals, we all need to find a reflection of ourselves somewhere, in someone else, so we can get to know ourselves and awaken our own consciousness. And hence the pressing need for a new and more conscious leadership to give us guidance and move us away from the outdated, narrow and inadequate leadership habits of the old paradigm.

Conscious leadership can manifest itself as a single individual within a team, or as a team within an organization, or as an organization within a society and, why not, as a society in the world. We know from experience how invaluable and transformative a true and conscious leader can be. It is wonderful to see change is possible. Evolution is unstoppable when their energy is transmitted to the team and then spreads to other teams, until the entire organization undergoes an astonishing transformation process.

It is not our intention here to define categorically the profile of a conscious leader, but simply to share our vision. It has to be a person of integrity, honest, connected with himself and with the world, sensitive to nature as a whole. He must be in love with life and interested in all people regardless of their origin and condition. Not a neo-romantic, but a person with common sense, grounded in his values, strong and clear in his convictions, a seeker and speaker of truth. Someone committed to his own personal growth and determined to help others by offering support, freedom and respect. Someone who follows his intuition intelligently and for the benefit of all. Above all, a visionary and courageous person, with the drive to take sensible risks and to make his contribution to a higher purpose. In this pursuit, he lives a coherent personal life. In his career, he will be leading a task, a project, a team, an organization, or a political party. Whatever the job, he is seen as an agent for change, but wears the burden lightly and with modesty, someone committed to the idea of a better world.

The critical situation today demands action; a step forward. A step to be taken by those who feel somehow moved by, and reflected in this profile, in what they are and in what they strive to be, who believe there is important and authentic work to be done. We need real change agents who are strong and passionate, acting as truly integral entrepreneurs economically, socially and environmentally.

In our experience, many people in positions of all kinds (CEOs, business owners, general managers, technicians or operators) fit this profile of Conscious Leader. In fact, we dare to say most people would fit into it. And the reason is that people are, above all, people. That is, once we soften some of the masks and armor we all wear, once we strip away some of the old organizational dynamics, once we offer a higher purpose, we find people who are, by definition, capable of a full and comprehensive expression of their four components explained above.

Who wouldn't choose to live in a better world? And who wouldn't do something about it if he could choose to do so? Conscious leaders can connect naturally with that part of themselves and decide to do their best to be happier and help others. They are aware of their own life and of what depends on them. And they are many, or maybe they are all of us. In fact, everything is in our hands. As Gandhi said, "You may never know what results come of your actions, but if you do nothing, there will be no results."

Lance Secretan, famous worldwide for his innovative contributions to the field of leadership, reveals his unique vision of conscious leadership in his latest work, *"One: The art and pratice of conscious leadership"* [45]. It is a thought-provoking essay highlighting the fact that whenever we experience pain or sadness, it is because we have been separated from what we love. And when we are inspired and joyful, it is because we are ONE with them. All human challenges and successes, he tells us, can be explained through this consciousness, which is the means to realize our greatness. We know from experience that it may sound bold for many to raise these issues in a 'management committee'. But the truth is there is always a way for those willing to make a move, to bring more awareness into an organization. The ideas in Secretan's book have been integrated into 30 of *Fortune's Most Admired Companies* and 11 of *Fortune's Best Companies to Work for in America*.

There is no reason to continue to separate human values from business effectiveness, to see them as being naturally in conflict with each other. It is important always to ask ourselves: "being effective for what?" According to Kofman [46], effectiveness is a measure that depends on the target; it is not an independent measure or entity in its own right. Unless we think about our goals, it makes no sense to ask ourselves if we are being effective. Unfortunately, most people act thoughtlessly from habit, without ever really considering their true aspirations or goals. But for those who have converge on the goals of happiness, fulfillment, freedom, peace and love – the same values at the core of all the world's wisdom traditions. So transcendent effectiveness can only be measured as the achievement of these objectives. As obvious as it may sound, Kofman points out that we all need reminding from time to time that success, money, achievements and other objects (whether physical, emotional, intellectual or spiritual) are means, not fundamental values. Values are concerned with the dimension of being; with who we are and how we behave to others. Values are not concerned with the dimension of having; with what objects we have acquired relative to others. We believe that the true source of satisfaction is the ability to experience essential states of happiness, fulfillment, freedom, peace and love with complete awareness.

The modern man spends most of the day at work, more time than doing any other activity or indeed the sum of all other activities when we are awake. Work is the 'chess board' where fulfillment and misery play out their old game. They are black pieces against white and we need to choose where we stand. Work is a scenario where every human can develop consciousness. When this development is aligned towards higher purpose and values, work becomes a work of art, a labour of love and a place of freedom and expression. When it is governed by unconscious habits and vices, it can be hell, a swamp of suffering and slavery.

While a senior in an organization has more "response-ability" (that is, ability to respond) than a manager or a line employee, we believe that anyone can take the position of conscious leader. We could all respond more consciously to those matters affecting us. Anyone connecting with, and living out the core values quoted above will have a transforming influence on their environment. The minute we take on this attitude and responsibility, any of us can be a change agent of the new paradigm of business.

We want to conclude this chapter with an excerpt of the speech Robert F. Kennedy gave at the University of Kansas in 1968, in his campaign for the presidency of the United States [47]:

"Too much and for too long, we seemed to have surrendered personal excellence and community values in the mere accumulation of material things. Our Gross National Product (GNP) ... -if we judge the United States of America by that, counts air pollution and cigarette advertising, and ambulances to clear our highways of carnage. It counts special locks for our doors and the jails for the people who break them. It counts the destruction of the redwood and the loss of our natural wonder in chaotic sprawl. It counts napalm [48] and counts nuclear

THE META-MODEL OF CONSCIOUS LEADERSHIP

warheads and armored cars for the police to fight the riots in our cities … Yet the gross national product does not allow for the health of our children, the quality of their education or the joy of their play. It does not include the beauty of our poetry or the strength of our marriages, the intelligence of our public debate or the integrity of our public officials. It measures neither our wit nor our courage, neither our wisdom nor our learning, neither our compassion nor our devotion to our country, it measures everything in short, except that which makes life worthwhile."

Organizational Prosperity

Organizational prosperity is the third and final basic principle of the Meta-Model of Conscious Leadership. This concept connects directly with some of the material in previous chapters, like 'Planet Earth in Transformation' and 'Social and Environmental Sustainability' in the first part of the book. Likewise, it is based on the universal concepts of *a systemic view* and *an integral vision of existence*, discussed above.

When we talk about business or organizational success, many will think immediately of economic benefits. And of course, these are part of prosperity because if a project is not economically sustainable, it will not last. Yet there are other factors of prosperity included in its definition. There is social prosperity: the organization should also contribute at a social level, treating the employee as a person, and seeking, as we said above, the balance between the four dimensions of existence. Social prosperity should also include the impact of our organization on society. Are we doing a social good? Are we hiring a representation of society, with their gender, age, ability, race and culture majorities and minorities? Does it provide real value beyond simply promoting more mindless consumption? Does it help or hinder in making the world a better place?

Finally, the third key element of organizational prosperity is the integration and respect for the environment. In previous sections we emphasized the importance of viewing our personal and professional activities and the environment as parts of a whole. Thus, respect for the environment means respect for ourselves.

We have already seen how globally relevant organizations such as the United Nations have adopted the principle of the *Triple Bottom Line* (TBL) to capture and expand the values and criteria by which we measure organizational (and social) success. In 2000 the UN proposed to measure corporate economic activity not only financially (*Profit*), but also socially (*People*) and environmentally (*Planet*). We refer to these three concepts as the three 'P's, shortened as 3P or P3, and they are part of our *raison d'être* as an organization.

Once we acknowledge that prosperity and success are much more than economic benefits, we can discuss how to increase this prosperity. How can a dedicated entrepreneur increase prosperity? Answering that question is the aim of Part IV of this book. But we can point out here the general lines of action for improvement and organizational growth. Organizations wanting to survive and thrive in the new business paradigm must have a longer-term perspective and focus on solving problems at their root rather than just patching over their symptoms. This is what we call organizational healing.

Organizational Healing

Modern medicine pursues the cure of specific diseases or specific problems, often without looking at the body as a whole, interrelated system. This form of curing is about patching, as does not seek solutions from the root. Similarly, the most common traditional business management approaches aim to detect and isolate the symptoms and act directly on them through specific and limited measures. For example, if overhead costs are very high, people are fired or salaries are lowered. And if we do not reach the sales targets, we increase the marketing budget and/or change the head of sales. This management approach, in the best of cases, just provides short-term results – the overhead costs creep up again because nothing really changed in the way work was done. Or the head of the sales team was replaced by a new head of sales while sales continue to disappoint. In fact, corporate management has developed over the last 100 years seeking excellence in the short-term and using patching as the main strategy, sometimes once and again.

In contrast more traditional medicine has effective diagnostic and intervention techniques that view and treat the human body holistically, considering health as a property of the body as a whole. Our business intervention methodology also seeks to develop healthy organizations and teams that function well not just within the team, but crucially with the rest of their organization. A healthy organization should have no problem balancing and achieving its short, medium and long-term goals. With this health status, it is better equipped to weather external difficulties. The body will remain healthy and it will not fall prey to the many diseases that claim enterprises whose body is out of balance because the treatment has focused only on local symptoms.

Acting in pursuit of a healthy organization is quite different from acting to cure specific symptoms and diseases. These two paradigms or different views of approaching organizational prosperity involve different actions and results, but are not necessarily mutually exclusive. It may be positive to both seek the overall healing of the organization and intervene directly on a particular symptom if it is too late to heal. It must certainly be unpleasant to have heart surgery because we smoked too much, but when we are faced with this situation, quitting will not solve the problem in the short term. So healing is more preventive than curative. But it is funny that companies who are doing better are also more aware that they need to continue investing in their health. In fact, it is not surprising. Isn't it the same with people?

Unlike curing, organizational healing takes a systemic view of the organization (as opposed to mechanistic), which implies a proactive effort. And this means, among other things, aligning employees around a common purpose, fostering cooperation and creativity, seeking the sustainability of our business, and pursuing personal motivation and commitment with a forward-looking vision.

We see this healing process or organizational improvement as a transformational journey which cannot be done in a day and needs effort and investment. If we think of the challenges most organizations are facing today, we can clearly see that they need this transformational process.

Just like humans cannot change their behavioral patterns without questioning their mental patterns, transformational change in an organization should also act at a deeper level in order to be truly transformational. Beliefs, values, identity and corporate culture must be changed. These deep levels organize and define more the more obvious levels, which are the skills and behaviors of individuals and teams. Affecting people's behaviors is the ultimate interest of all change management practices; to obtain different results we have to do things differently. So, when we are able to modify organizations at a deep level, real behavioral changes arise naturally in the surface levels. In this way, the change is incorporated into both the organization and its individuals and it is solid and sustainable over time.

Let us see a couple of simple examples: in order to get an internal process to be followed (behavior), it is more effective and lasting to change participants' beliefs such as 'the process is necessary and helps us all' rather than to press with short-term incentives or threats so that the process is used.

If we are seeking to achieve changes in the way our people communicate (behavior), it is also more effective and durable to drive adoption of the belief 'my colleagues and collaborators deserve all my respect and attention' than to offer a course in effective communication. The only way to really change long-term behavior is acting in these deeper levels (beliefs, values, identity, culture...).

This transformation of the organization is a journey that takes time. It is a process that must be walked step by step. It must be worked and cannot be bought. It is not a document saying what to do or how things must be. It is a process that has to be an authentic experience for every person in the organization, starting with those in higher positions. It is not just a mission 'for the others'. And like any change meant to be deep and sustainable, this transformational process involves significant effort and often some sacrifices.

We now conclude this section, still conceptual and with a significant degree of abstraction. However, it was important for us to lay the general foundation supporting our methodology. In the next three parts we will put all these concepts into practice, giving real examples and specific guidelines on how to develop the required changes in organizations of all kinds; large and small, public and private.

In summary, the Meta-Model interprets reality in a specific way and in an organizational framework through two levels of ideas / concepts:

Universal Concepts:
- Everything is Energy (everything and everyone is a form of energy).
- Systemic View (of the organization, the team, the world...).
- Integral Vision of Existence (physical, mental, emotional and spiritual).

Fundamental Principles:
- Conscious Leadership (the 21st century needs a new leader).
- Living Organizations (organizations are also living organisms).
- Organizational Prosperity (the 3Ps: Profit, People, Planet).

PART III

ORGANIZATIONAL ENERGY SYSTEM (OES)®

- The Chakras
- Chakra 1: GROUNDING
- Chakra 2: WELLBEING
- Chakra 3: WILLPOWER
- Chakra 4: COOPERATION
- Chakra 5: EXPRESSION
- Chakra 6: WISDOM
- Chakra 7: COMMUNITY

The Chakras

Chakra comes from the Sanskrit word *cakra*, meaning wheel or disc. It refers to the circular form in which the energy moves in an energetic center. The 7 human chakras form a metaphysical system that shapes the relationship between the different aspects of human existence. It has its roots in concepts of yoga practice originating in India thousands of years ago. These 7 centers, distributed along the axis of the spine, are activity centers for the reception, assimilation and transmission of vital energies. Each chakra is associated with a specific psychological function and they are all connected through an energy channel that runs along the entire spine.

Many authors have written about the chakra system, also known as the Human Energy System. Yoga and meditation practitioners have a more developed awareness of these energy centers. But we all know from intuition that our body is full of energy and that how we manage this energy is vital to our performance. In an article published by the *Harvard Business Review* entitled "Manage Your Energy, Not Your Time" [49], Schwartz and McCarthy clearly conveyed this idea for managers and executives to get the most out of this vital energy within our reach. We all have times when we feel tired and cranky and times when everything seems to be on our side. Whether we are aware or not, this is a direct consequence of how energy flows inside us.

In Part II of the book we looked at the energetic reality of our world and of individuals in particular. Work teams, departments, business units and organizations of any kind are made up by people. They have the power of the collective. This energy depends not only on individual energies, but on other external factors that might have an influence on it. Let us set an example: a business where all the employees have to clock in every morning for control reasons will have a certain kind of energy, different from an organization where the employees are trusted to do their best for themselves and for the company. Likewise, an organization that has sports facilities where the employees can exercise will have a different kind of energy from an organization where working conditions are hard and even the lights are too dim to make our eyes work comfortably.

We can think of another example of an organization where the staff respect and even praise each others' differences. This has a positive effect on employee motivation. On the other hand, there are organizations where diversity is not a value and individuals are discriminated based on gender, race or skills. Every organization can reach a state of positive energy when all the employees are aligned towards a common vision and there is trust and cooperation between them. This can lead to a higher degree of prosperity compared to an organization where the vision is not clear and accepted and there is no real trust and partnership between its workers. These more positive or less positive effects are just healthy or not so healthy energy states in an organization. This is a very intuitive and yet powerful concept that we can use to improve the energy system of our organizations and its performance. As with the human chakras, the organizational chakras or energy centers may be deficient in some aspects and excessive in others. The excessive activity of a chakra is an imbalance that tries to make up for the deficiency in other aspects of the energetic body.

In his book: "Leading at a higher level" [50], Ken Blanchard says that high-performance organizations have systems and energy-generating structures, rather than policies and procedures that may hinder employee performance to serve their customers effectively.

The new concept of the Organizational Energy System (OES)® refers to the energy in an organization or organizational energy body. This energy exists and it can be more or less positive. It can flow well or be blocked. Obviously, the different areas or functions of an organization will also have different energies. In fact, they are different energy bodies. For example: let's take a company operating in 5 countries and organized around two business units; The whole organization is a body or energy system that is the sum of its members. In turn, each of the five geographies is an energy body in its own right with its own challenges and strengths. And the same applies for the two business units. The main purpose of this book is to explore how we can analyze, understand and harness these energies to improve our organization, that is, to achieve higher levels of prosperity. In this section we will explain the concept of the Organizational Energy System. This is the basis for the fourth part of this book, where we present a unique and innovative methodology for organizational healing.

In the next section we will assess the 7 human chakras one by one and establish parallelisms with the organization. We have relied on several authors, highlighting the work of Anodea Judith, one of the reference authors who has been researching and documenting the chakras and the human energy system for years. Judith has written several books like: "Wheels of Life", "The Chakra System", "Eastern Body, Western Mind", and "The Sevenfold Journey: Reclaiming Mind, Body & Spirit Through the Chakras" [51], among others.

We have noticed minor variations in the interpretation of human chakras depending on the author and the specific focus of the book. Our selection here is meant to be integrative rather than exclusive. We especially liked the clarity and depth Anodea Judith uses to describe the seven energy centers. We have also relied on other recognized authors like Ambika Wauters ("*The book of Chakras*") [52], Laura Tuan ("*The Great Book of the Chakras*") [53], Barbara A. Brennan, ("*Hands of Light*") [54] and Caroline Myss audio books ("*Exploring Chakras*" and "*The Energetics of Healing*").

In this second edition of *Organizational Energy*, we want to acknowledge Peter ten Hoopen and Fons Trompenaars for their book: *"The Enlightened Leader, an introduction to the chakras of leadership"*; a book that applied the human chakra system to an organizational setting, although focusing on the individual leader instead of the organization. While this book was not part of our initial inspiration, we were happy to see that it defends some of the same concepts and principles of sustainability and humanism that we do in this publication. In their words: *"There is growing consensus [...] that we are in need of a fundamental transformation of the way we do business."* It is a passionate, provocative and sometimes amuzing read that we highly recommend.

Additionally, it was encouraging to see the close parallelism between the way ten Hoopen and Trompenaars applied the chakra model to business and leadership and how we have conceptualized the organizational energy system (the organizational chakras). Our publication, however, is not to be seen as a port of arrival –it is the beginning of a process in our constant research on organizational chakras that we have committed to pursue. The aim is to develop a system that reflects reality and to condense it in a simple model for the entrepreneur, the business and the organizational world.

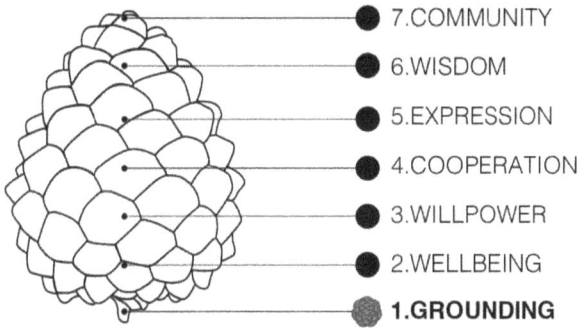

- 7.COMMUNITY
- 6.WISDOM
- 5.EXPRESSION
- 4.COOPERATION
- 3.WILLPOWER
- 2.WELLBEING
- **1.GROUNDING**

Chakra 1: GROUNDING

The concept in human beings

The Sanskrit word for this charka is *Muladhara*, which means "root". Its element is the "Earth", firm and solid.

The first chakra represents our roots, foundations and physical body; and also our survival instinct, which stimulates the aggressive instincts related to it. This chakra strengthens our spirit on a material level and sets the foundations of our human existence. It also governs the process of birth and our early years: the core of our identity. Our purpose is to build a solid basis that supports our subsequent work in life. If we have deep, strong roots, we can bring stability, health and strength to our body and live.

When this chakra is healthy, our survival instinct and sense of belonging are strong and we feel a greater sense of security. But if this chakra is weak or damaged, achieving this feeling of security and grounding can become an ordeal.

This chakra is activated in times of stress or crisis, helping us fight and compete. It is our survival instinct that is activated.

Parallelism in the organization

The interpretation of this chakra in the organization is clear. It represents the overall health of its foundational basis and the strength of its roots to ensure survival, growth and prosperity. Each organizational chakra is structured around three main angles for a thorough analysis of its global implications. In this case, the first assesses whether the foundational energy is present today, the second analyzes the real value added we bring to the market, and the third focuses on the resources available and our financial health. These three components of Grounding are analyzed separately below.

Foundational Energy:

The foundational moment of any living organism is of paramount importance: when, where and how it took place will have an influence on its life. Take for example, a company created from a merger, it will not have the same foundational energy as a company that has been growing gradually and that was founded by two partners.

Foundational moments should be understood as the pillars of the organization and its identity. It is possible to re-set or to modify a building foundation, but it is rather expensive and complicated. At an organizational level, we need to understand to what extent this foundational moment is still present and the kind of energy it now brings to the organization, the managers, the employees and the whole world.

The systemic configurations that authors like Hellinger, Weber and Vargas have developed in recent years, and that we discussed in Part II, give great importance to the foundational moment of an organization. These authors support that factors like who the founder or founders were, who provided the money and the philosophy behind its foundation are vital to understanding the current dynamics, even many years after its foundation.

Many organizations are aware of this and out of intuition, common sense or respect, pay tribute to their founders and origins. They might set up an exhibition about their past with a display of historical photographs, open a museum or do other activities. If the foundational energy of an organization has not suffered dramatic changes, or if these are handled properly and respectfully, this foundational energy will empower the new generations of employees.

In summary, the first angle of the Grounding chakra assesses the strength that the foundational energy brings to the present moment.

Foundational Energy - Examples of good and poor performance:

Here are some examples that help us understand its application to the organizational reality. Organizations with a strong legacy and that pay tribute to their founders are those with a higher foundational energy. Some examples of organizations with strong foundational energy who have created exhibitions or museums are; Maersk, Lego, BMW and Apple.

On the other hand, there are companies that underestimate the importance of their foundation, or that have been through a period of crisis in their history. This is the case of most mergers and acquisitions, where an organization has to break with its roots and culture overnight to "fit into" another. It is like transplanting a tree. The older it is, the stronger the roots are and the more it is used to a type of soil, the chances of survival are smaller. Not surprisingly, after years of organizations merging, the success rate is below 50%. Yet this trend seems to be growing. It definitely has benefits: synergies, economies of scale, leading market positions or brand awareness. These are all important, but unless individuals and the organizational culture, intrinsically linked to the foundational roots of the organization, are taken care of, the merger will not be successful.

Value Added:

Similarly to what happens with trees and plants, the soil where an organizational body is rooted needs to be fertile. Our products and services will find fertile soil if there is a place in the market for what we do. That is, if we bring real value through our products and/or services.

If we cannot achieve the margins we need to operate, we should not blame it on others. The value we bring to the market does not only depend on external factors, like the life cycle of the products we offer or the market's inherent competitiveness. We need to assume our share of responsibility and search for the answers in our scope of action: have we followed a functionally and geographically diversified strategy? Have we invested enough in R&D and in due time? Have we managed operating costs so as to be competitive and bring value to the market? Do we offer the quality expected from our positioning?

Kim and Mauborgne popularized the concept of blue oceans [55] to refer to those untapped markets covering a basic customer need. Organizations that know how to find their blue oceans are providing maximum value. They can create fertile markets and enjoy higher margins than those surviving in red oceans, where competition is fierce and customers have all the power.

A company well diversified (in product, industry and geography) is like a tree with long roots that can reach far to provide all the necessary nutrients. If the tree does not get sufficient nutrients from one place, it will search somewhere else. There are shrubs that grow in the desert with minimal water, and they are very efficient systems that have adapted to a harsh reality to survive. Others need large amounts of water but have adapted to the cold. The important thing is to design our organization in line with what we are or want to be.

Another way of understanding this angle of the first organizational chakra is the 'right' of the organization to exist, its *raison d'etre*. Every organization, whether for or not for profit, should be able to discern the value it brings to the market and to the social fabric. If a company adds value, the market/society will provide the nutrients for its activity (fertility). Otherwise, the market or the society will marginalize and neglect it.

In summary, the second angle of the root chakra assesses the real value we bring to the market. In other words, it questions whether the market legitimates (with its fertility) what we are offering.

Value Added - Examples of good and poor performance:
Here are some examples to better understand these concepts in the world of business and organizations: *Le Cirque du Soleil* is an example of a company that created its own blue ocean when the circus market was competitive (red ocean) and in decline. They found a way to re-define the market creating a product that was closer to a Broadway musical or show than to a traditional circus. Nearly three decades after their birth, the company still creates great expectations in all of their shows around the world.

Another example of a company that found fertility in a competitive market is *IKEA*. As we all know, they reinvented the concept of furniture and home decor. There are many other examples we can think of like *SouthWest Airlines*, who invented the concept of "low-cost" flights, or *3M*, who created the concept of the "glue that does not stick", the *post-it*.

Business efficiency, productivity and quality are important factors when assessing our market value, but they are not always the most important ones. When a new market is created, the organizations that succeed are not those with lower costs, but those that are first to provide the new market need. Think of the Internet market and, more recently, the market of *Apps*. Still, when the market reaches maturity, companies that survive will be those with a better market positioning in terms of quality, technology or service. An example is *Apple*'s products. Another is *Amazon*, with a retail sales model that was ahead of its time and who will continue to grow further. On the contrary, if we lack a strong value positioning, we will compete in price amidst a red ocean. In in such scenarios, businesses will only survive if they can adapt their costs by developing economies of scale, increasing productivity and eliminating unnecessary system costs. Think of the many companies competing in the market of PCs or in the physical distribution of printed books.

There are organizations, like government or NGOs, where the concept of blue ocean is somewhat blurred. In this cases we can understand this value added as their right to exist. If we think, for example, of the police force of a sovereign state, there is no doubt that this organization is covering a market or social need, not intended to control or suppress citizens, but to ensure compliance with the fundamental human rights. Likewise, we can understand that the service provided by a public or private hospital brings real value to the market, as long as it is located in an area where there is real demand for the services offered.

On the other side of the spectrum are organizations that "have no right to exist"; which is something that the market, meaning all of us, decides. Here we can find companies offering technologically outdated products or services, like shops developing old photo reels, video stores, or fax machines. If companies like these rely on just one root, market or product, and fail to react on time and to reinvent themselves, diversify or internationalize, the land where they are rooted will gradually dry. Take the case of *Kodak*, a successful company that did not manage to adapt to the market changes on time.

We can also think of the recent over-exploitation in the real estate market. When the bubble burst, many companies were left without a place to survive. Some years ago these companies found a market where they could add value, then lost it and finally disappeared. This is poetic justice somehow; quite likely, the last to enter the real estate market had a speculative purpose rather than a real motivation to add value.

Available resources:

If the previous angle assessed the value we bring to the market, where we are rooted and whether it is fertile soil, this angle represents the amount of nutrients that come from that market.

This angle describes and assesses how we obtain the resources we need from the market. When we talk about resources, we mean not only the financial resources but also the physical assets (factories, machinery...) and the workforce. The financial health of an organization is vitally important; but a company can have healthy finances and still have outdated machinery, premises in a bad location, or an infrastructure unable to respond to the changing market needs. Similarly, a company with a positive EBITDA may have a workforce whose skills are no longer suited to their needs. In these changing times having a large staff of workers (especially in countries with inflexible labor markets) may become a burden instead of an engine.

Many conservative companies have decided to grow at a slower pace but without having to leverage their financial resources in excess. In a time of crisis, a company that has been conservative will have a greater chance to survive. We are not judging which financial policy is best, as long as an excessive desire for growth blind us and makes us contract financial leverage beyond our possibilities. In fact, economists have recently started to question whether if indeed companies should be in constant growth. And the truth is many companies are too eager to grow. We should ask ourselves: why do we need to grow so much? If the cells of the human body grow excessively where they should not, we call it cancer. A healthy sustained growth is better than a fast and uncontrolled one.

In summary, the third angle of the Grounding chakra assesses the amount of material, human and financial resources available to the company.

Available resources - Examples of good and poor performance:
Organizations with good financial resources operate in markets where they are in a situation of little competition (monopoly, oligopoly) and can afford to have high margins, or where they can add great value due to a technologically superior product, etc. This was the case of *HP* inkjet printers in the 80s, *Plantronics* wireless headphones in the 90s and, more recently, *Apple iphones* or *ipads*.

On the other hand, there are companies or organizations that cannot obtain enough resources to ensure their survival. Economic difficulties are one of the major business problems of all times, and of course in the recent global economic downturn. We all know many examples of companies with scarce economic resources.

For a non-profit organization, this angle also refers to the inflow of resources, whether they come from donations, subsidies, contributions from members or employers. Every organization, for and not for profit, needs vital resources to fund its activities.

Material resources have to do with the adequacy of the physical assets of the company to its business. Obviously, these translate into money, but in many cases they are long-term investments that prevent us from reacting in a timely fashion to a market change. In fact, quite often, the premises are not perfectly suited to our business needs. They might be too big because we have miss-estimated the demand we would have; or too small and with no chance of taking on more square meters quickly. Both cases can hinder our development. As a consequence, outsourcing services and contract manufacturing have rapidly grown, allowing us to focus on our core competences.

This angle also refers to human resources, even if we would rather not refer to people as "resources". There are increasingly less human resources (HR) managers and more managers of people and organizations. Many times the collective capabilities of the people in an organization are not suitable for its needs. In such cases, organizations need to adapt, and this is a constant variable in companies that survive over time. Any company operating for 50 years will have to adapt to the market in one way or another. Production lines that "move" from developed countries to areas where labor is cheaper, technological advances that require multi-skilled staff, important strategic twists like abandoning a market, sales, mergers, acquisitions, or legislation changes could all destabilize a business due to the inadequacy of its human capabilities and skills.

In 2010 the Spanish government changed the laws in the sector of the external labor risk prevention services. Until then, prevention services depended on labor insurance companies and could only offer their services to the holders of those insurances. They had a captive market as companies had to hire their services by law. In 2010 they issued the so-called law of independence that liberalized the sector. External prevention service companies had a highly qualified staff for technical and health related aspects of prevention but poorly qualified for the new challenges facing the market (client acquisition, marketing, satisfaction and loyalty management). In other words, the available resources they had were inadequate.

Grounding Chakra - The HP case:

After looking at the three angles of the first organizational chakra, we will analyze a real example, the case of *Hewlett-Packard*.

Founded in 1939, Hewlett-Packard (HP) started selling technologically advanced products to improve the value chain of other organizations (Business-to-Business: B2B), like oscilloscopes and signal analyzers. They grew steadily by diversifying their portfolio of products and services to include calculators, printers and laptops for domestic use (Business-to-Consumer: B2C).

For many years the founders Bill Hewlett and Dave Packard worked at the organization setting the example of the foundational values that had made their venture a very successful multinational corporation. Their products clearly provided a market value and were therefore fertile. This also resulted in a good availability of material, financial and human resources. HP attracted some of the best professionals. It was a conservative organization, made of engineers, as it was said inside the company.

At one point they hired the first external CEO in their history. She had a vision of making Hewlett-Packard a FMCG company. From then onwards, Hewlett-Packard decided to promote their initials HP and dumped (via spin-off) the foundational business to business (B2B) original product lines. It was then renamed to Agilent Technologies. In the process, it acquired another big multinational (Compaq) to reinforce the B2C business. This was a highly controversial decision that divided the board, with the son of one of the founders opposing the move.

Perhaps this new strategy made sense on paper, but it neglected key aspects like the foundational moment of the business and the energy it brought to the present day. The spreadsheet evoked attractive economic forecasts, however, it overlooked the essential part of the organization's roots and the corporate culture that had brought together thousands of professionals for years. What was meant to be a controlled movement of people, business units, products and processes left thousands of workers in the company confused and angry. From then on, HP was no longer meant to be a company of engineers, but of marketeers.

More than 10 years after these changes, the company has still not recovered the vital energy it once had. HP is a company that meant a lot to all it's people and still produces millions of good products every month. It has a very acceptable economic performance, but it is no longer one of the most valued in terms of job recruitment. The 2010 annual survey conducted by the company in one of the most desired HP divisions and geographies revealed that over 70% of the employees would leave the company to work elsewhere with a similar compensation level. And this is an undesirable situation for any organization. It is not by chance that companies like Google or Apple today are ahead in the game as 'the most desirable places to work'.

We are not saying here that there should not be spin-offs or changes in the strategic direction of the company, but that these should be done with conscience and respect for the universal laws governing the foundational order. As we mentioned in previous sections, there are state-of-the-art techniques that help to understand the systemic effects in these difficult transitions.

The other two angles of the first chakra, value added and available resources, were energies that had been flowing well in the past: HP products found a well-deserved fertility because they contributed real value. After they moved to the consumer market, emphasis was on volume and cost control rather than on product quality. There was pressure, real or fictional, from financial analysts to report positive quaterly growth rates and generous profitability. It seemed that Bill Hewlett and Dave Packard's long-term project had become a shortsighted opportunistic company. All this affected more angles of the other chakras in the organizational energy system. As a result, the company went from an international benchmark to a business (albeit very large) that had lost its way in a very short period of time.

Summary - GROUNDING chakra:

Angles	What is assessed?
Foundational energy	The strength that the foundational energy provides to the present moment.
Value added	The real value we bring to the market and the fertility we can find in it.
Available resources	The amount of material, human and financial resources the company has available.

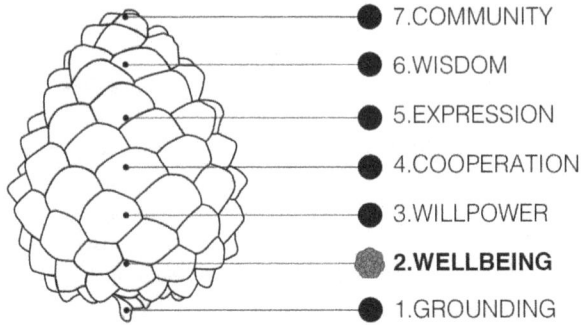

7.COMMUNITY
6.WISDOM
5.EXPRESSION
4.COOPERATION
3.WILLPOWER
2.WELLBEING
1.GROUNDING

Chakra 2: WELLBEING

The concept in human beings

This chakra is called *Svadhisthana* in Sanskrit, which literally means "sweetness". Its element is "water", fluid and flexible.

If we have a solid first chakra, our foundations will be strong and will allow us to expand without losing our center. While the first chakra referred to the stability given by strong roots, the second chakra refers to movement and change. Movement promotes health and body flexibility, releasing energy that might be locked. This movement is also a movement of emotions. Emotions can be seen as a reaction to pleasure and pain. Pain can appear as a consequence to something that threatens our survival. And when the body experiences pain, we are not emotionally fit and we tend to suppress our feelings and sensations. Our efforts focus on keeping things as they are and we resist change.

Instead, when survival is guaranteed, the body naturally focuses on pleasure, one of the main characteristics of this chakra. When we feel good and emotionally safe, we are able to experience pleasure. Then we tend to relax and we can allow ourselves to flow energetically, to expand and to work to our maximum potential.

If the second chakra is energetically poor, there will be fear of change, lack of creativity and we will focus on the structural realities of the first chakra. This translates into the lack of emotional expression or lack of sensuality. If this chakra is too open, we observe an excess of emotions, constantly changing from one extreme to the other.

The emotions and "sweetness" associated with pleasure lead to sexuality, one of the basic components of this chakra. It is the equivalent to being attractive to others. The governing force of this chakra is the attraction of the opposites comfort vs. conflict, adaptability v. rigidity, and attractiveness vs. indifference).

Parallelism in the organization

The interpretation of this chakra in the organization leads us to several concepts: the emotional state of the employees and how this affects interpersonal relationships in the organization, the adaptability of the organization during transitions and the attraction our brand can generate in the market. Here we see that the translation of human chakras into the organizational world applies to both, the living organism itself as well as its workers. People could be seen here as the organizational cells, an essential part of the organizational energy. Thus, we have defined the three angles of this chakra as the employees' emotions (comfort and conflict), the adaptability to change in the organization as a whole (vs. rigidity) and its image in the market (attractiveness vs. indifference). Creativity and innovation, a key aspect of any organization's prosperity in time, which could be argued to also reside in this chakra, has been conceptualized as a composite of several chakras. For instance the level of cooperation, the quality of our communication, the effectiveness of our decision making processes and our values will all affect how we translate our creative ideas into product/service or process innovations.

Emotions:
The first angle of this chakra refers to the emotions of workers and collaborators within the system. When there is "pleasure" and comfort at work, people feel at ease interacting with others, they are happy and motivated, and they are willing to give the best of themselves. When people feel respected and valued (regardless of their origin, appearance, religious beliefs, age, gender, etc.) and they have the knowledge and the skills to do their job, they can flow, contribute ideas, collaborate with others and develop their full potential. As we see, valuing diversity is an intrinsic aspect of the emotional state of employees at work. When all this is met, there will be real employee commitment and productive interpersonal relationships.

However, when "pain", discrimination and conflict arise in our organization, motivation for being part of the project will be low. The conflict here is to be understood as negative, and therefore as personal and destructive. As Bernal explains in his article "Team Diversity" [56], not all forms of conflict are bad, since difference of opinion is absolutely necessary in order to take full advantage of the diversity in a team. But destructive conflict, affecting someone's emotions negatively, will be a hindrance to our efficiency, productivity and organizational prosperity in general. It is also a deterrent for people to express their innate creativity.

This angle includes "climate surveys" or satisfaction workforce indicators. Unfortunately these diagnostic tools have been used unwisely by many organizations and now many people are somewhat skeptical about what it will be done with the results of such studies.

In an organization where this angle is strong, people can easily express their emotions (rather than suppress them) and be their authentic selves. It is obvious that this expression will also depend on cultural traits since Asians, for instance, do not express themselves the same way as Latinos.

In summary, the first angle of the Wellbeing chakra assesses the emotional climate of all workers in the organization and how this translates into interpersonal relationships.

Emotions - Examples of good and poor performance

The *Google* project, started by Larry Page and Sergey Brin in late 1998, has become an organizational reference for many people. If you still have not seen the videos about the organization and the good employee relationship, just type "*Working at google*" on *YouTube* and enjoy it. Clearly, there are not many companies like *Google* in terms of business success and innovation in people management processes (formerly, human resource management, HRM). *Google* found inspiration in management models led by *Hewlett-Packard, IBM* and other American corporations and took it to the next level. Not all organizations can (or should) create workspaces like *Google* has, but they can adopt its essence: respect for the individual, trust and work-life balance. When we believe that people are naturally good, we are confident they will do their job the best they can and we will help them reach their full potential. It is just common sense. Is there any young graduate (or not so young) who would not like to work for *Google*?

The opposite happens in companies that do not trust their workers and they establish a culture of control. And here we prefer not to give any specific examples, but there are many. We can also find organizations where workers are the ones who do not trust their leaders. If we are experiencing downsizing processes, closing factories, selling divisions or mergers, the tendency will be job insecurity and mistrust. The result is likely to be an emotionally upset workforce, unable to develop their full potential. In some extreme cases, employees' performance is not just below their capacities (80, 50 or 20%), but they could be contributing with a negative percentage, affecting the environment and the motivation of other partners negatively. The hallway conversations or hearsay are a favorite pastime in companies that are emotionally unstable. Would any young graduate like to work for a company like that? Later in this chapter we will see how we can improve these emotions and personal anxieties through better communication (fifth chakra).

Adaptability to change:

All living bodies need constant adaption to the environment. And this is especially true for organizations that want to exist for decades in the current changing reality. It is surprising that the life expectancy of large multinational corporations (*Fortune 500* type) is only between 40 and 50 years [37]. A too rigid structure will apparently provide support, but when the ground beneath us moves, it will break like concrete breaks with an earthquake. In seismic zones like California, buildings are made of wood, iron or new and more flexible construction materials "to adjust" to the tremors.

We need strong roots to stay grounded to who we are and where we came from (first chakra). Then the organization will have to adapt to the current social and economic reality. This adaptability is one of the key aspects of individual and organizational creativity. Structures that are rigid and over-proceduralized will never lead to creative actions.

Thus, adaptability to change in an organization depends on the rigidity of its structure and its people. Organizational charts that have not changed for long tend to develop inefficiencies and store diseases: some can create little fiefdoms and the purpose of the "common good" can be lost in favor of "my own good and that of my people". Personal rigidity is related to the mental structures of individuals, strongly conditioned by the prevailing corporate culture. When faced with personal change, egos and fears arise. And these are two major deterrents of creativity and organizational adaptability.

In summary, the second angle of the Wellbeing chakra assesses to what extent our organization adapts to change.

Adaptability to change - Examples of good and poor performance

Now consider the case of an army. Adaptability refers to the flexible organizational structures that adapt to the changing environment; the market. We have seen many armies that have adapted to a more up-to-date interpretation of the concept of citizen rights defense. As we saw in the section "The planet Earth in transformation", the U.S. Military is trying to anticipate and prepare for the potential effects of climate change on civilians.

Of course, this adaptability to change will somehow depend on the industry in which we operate. For example, in the car industry, with product cycles of 3-5 years, it will be more difficult to adapt to the market rapidly. But within each sector, what determines whether an organization is more or less flexible is the flexibility of its leaders and the organization's structures and processes. It is important to mention here that the OES is a systemic model and as such, all elements are interconnected and interrelated. As an example, there are other elements in higher chakras that will impact on the organizations' ability to adapt, like how we communicate internally (chakra 5), or how we manage and incorporate new knowledge (chakra 6).

If we go long without "listening" to the market, most likely new companies will be created and displace us. We mentioned before the example of *Cirque du Soleil* as an organization that could create its blue ocean where there was no competition. Could "traditional" circuses have been able to adapt to what the market wanted?

An example of adaptability to change is the case of *Telefónica de España S.A.*, the national operator that held the monopoly on communications in Spain for years. After two critical situations that affected the market and the industry, they demonstrated intelligence and adaptability. Today they remain the largest telecom operator in Spain and they also have a strong presence in South America. *Telefónica* was able to adapt to the liberalization of the telecom market with the consequent entry into the Spanish territory of other powerful European operators like *Vodafone, France Telecom, British Telecom* or *Orange*. They also took advantage of the migration of telecommunication landlines to mobile and Internet services. In this adaptation process ending in transformation, *Telefónica* changed its name to that of the subsidiary created for mobiles, *Movistar*.

Brand image:

The third and final angle of the second organizational chakra is represented by our brand image. How attractive are we to others? Can we attract talent, build partnerships with other organizations in the value chain, and appeal to our customers? As with the human body, our sensuality as an 'organizational body' is a reflection of our inner health and wellbeing. "The face is the reflection of the soul", says the proverb. Then, what is our organizational "face" the reflection of? Here we find concepts such as brand awareness: Is it known? Where and where not? How do the different markets or interest groups see us? What is our organization associated with? Maybe with quality, speed or low cost. If we ask the market all these questions and listen objectively, we will understand what our image and market positioning are.

In summary, the third angle of the Wellbeing chakra assesses our brand image in the markets where we operate.

Brand image - Examples of good and poor performance

Each year *BrandZ* publishes a ranking of the most valued brands. In 2011, and for the first time after this analysis was released, *Apple* ranked first with an increase of 84% over the previous year ahead of *Google*, who had held the top spot since 2007.

People travel from miles around to find an *Apple* store and spend twice the amount they would invest in functionally similar alternatives. Let us leave this debate open and look at the objective result, people are willing to buy that particular brand for a number of reasons.

Now think of the opposite end. Make a list of three companies that not only have a bad image, but where you have avoided buying in the past for whatever reason. Those are just a few examples you can judge for yourselves.

Let us try this next: what is your reaction when you think of the following organizations? Take some time to notice how your body reacts to each of them: *IKEA, Iberia, Microsoft, Johnson&Johnson, L'Oreal, Nike, Mercedes, Corona, NATO, Allianz, American Airlines, British Petroleum, General Motors, Whole Foods, Nestle, Pinea3.* When we know a brand, we all have a picture of it. That image, however questionable, is our reality based on personal experiences or what we have read or been told. But one thing is clear: we do have that image, wherever it comes from.

If our brand image is not known and recognized, we will gravitate towards a price war as the only differentiator among the various market players. Think of highly fragmented markets, where individual positioning is not critical for consumers to choose the brand and what it represents: wine, paper, tires, or a cable. In fact, in all markets we can see movements of these players, leaders, standing out by improving their brand image.

Billions of Euros have been spent positioning brands without a real desire to be what they convey. Did you know that the facial muscles necessary to make a fake smile are different from those used to make a real smile? [57]. Similarly, markets and all of us can perceive when a company is honest and consistent and when it is just inspiration from the marketing department. Is there any organization that does not deserve the image we have of it?

Well-being Chakra – The Montesa case

We will now explore the case of *Montesa*, a company with its ups and downs that is a good example to illustrate the different angles of the second chakra: emotions, adaptability to change and brand image.

Montesa was a Spanish motorcycle manufacturer whose origins date back to 1944, when Pere Permanyer turned its automotive gas generator industry to the motorcycle industry. During the Second World War (1939-45) and the reconstruction after the Spanish Civil War (1936-39), the fuel shortage had crippled transportation in Spain. Thus, the application of the gasogene system (a skillful procedure for burning almond shells to obtain lean gas as fuel), was almost a magical resource for running cars, trucks and power generators. In 1944, with the expected end of Second World War, Permanyer anticipated that the fuel supply would soon go back to normal and that he would have to therefore reorient his industry to another activity. His first idea was to study a two-stroke engine for motorcycles. In those days there was extraordinary demand for this type of light vehicles and a total lack of self-production and imports. Thus, *Montesa's* adaptability to circumstances became evident and proved to be the reason for its foundation.

Pere Permanyer and Paco Bultó met during the Spanish Civil War reuniting tow complementary vocations: Permanyer's industrial vocation and Bultó's technical-sportive. This is how the brand was born out of two founding partners. Joan Cañellas, *Montesa's* CEO until it closed as an independent company in 1987, explained to us in an interview that the company had three clearly differentiated stages: the foundational, in a Spanish of economic autarky, the internationalization, with imports and exports, and the era of globalization, with the incorporation of *Honda* to the group.

During the first stage, tensions emerged between the founding partners and in 1958 they decided to split up. Permanyer preferred to leave the competition because of the financial difficulties, while Bultó called

ORGANIZATIONAL ENERGY SYSTEM (OES)®

for a gradual abandonment so as to keep the commitments with racers and races. As he could not reach an agreement with the Board of Directors of *Montesa*, Bultó sold his shares and created *Bultaco*, a company *Montesa* would compete with thereafter. As Cañellas told us, "the break was emotionally traumatic for the partners. It was also traumatic for workers, who had to decide who they wanted to follow. Permanyer had to restructure the management team after most of the technical staff left to Bultaco. He showed his leadership and perseverance once again. He managed to overcome the difficult situation and to create a solid company that reached a size of 500 employees. They had offices in many foreign countries and launched successful motorcycle models, like the *Impala* and *Cota*.

The 60s were some pretty good years. The *Impala* was a long series product. About 25,000 units (all the same) were produced every year. *Montesa* was a solid company: modern, prestigious, high-tech and with a good brand image. "Things were done with a long-term vision and the idea to last, not like now," says Cañellas. The brand was based on the concepts of service, quality and price, in that order. It was a period of comfort for the company and its workers. There was always an excuse to open a bottle of champagne to celebrate a race or any other event.

But this boom period was followed by difficulties. The *Impala* slowly faded with the launch of *SEAT 600* cars and Montesa had to cut down its production to sports bikes only: trial, motocross, enduro… (with less units and more models and colors). They reorganized, invested in IT and developed the engine block, but they had a technological limitation with a small domestic market. Even if they exported more than 50% of their production, Japanese brands like *Honda* and *Yamaha* had far better economies of scale. In the 70s the Japanese were steadily growing worldwide. While *Montesa* sold between fifteen and twenty thousand bikes a year (counting all countries and models), *Honda* sold four million. "With these synergies they managed to do the same we did but better, nicer and cheaper," says Cañellas. There was a short-term risk for *Montesa,* especially in the U.S., where 40% of the production was exported and the Japanese were growing rapidly. *Honda* sold their models at about 300 dollars, while *Montesa*, with higher costs, had to sell their bikes at around 500 dollars.

To avoid excessive dependence on the American territory, they decided to diversify the market geographically: England, France, Italy, Germany, other European countries, and any other solvent country even small or distant that could become a selling point, from Reunion Islands to New Zealand. Thus, American exports went down by 10% and they focused on other countries where *Montesa* could still find a fertile market. Two years later, the American market collapsed making *Bultaco* and *Ossa*, who had not diversified geographically, go burst.

It was the 80s and *Montesa* was still alive, but not for long. They had to negotiate a joint-venture with *Honda* in Spain. This was emotionally another litmus test for the company's workers and especially for Permanyer and his son-in-law Cañellas. The dependence relationship with *Honda* was a dramatic experience. Cañellas tells us that in those difficult days he would spend two hours every morning in the R&D Department: "It was the place that gave me the emotional balance I needed to face the day and somehow recharge the original spirit of the company."

Ossa and *Bultaco* had closed leaving many people unemployed. Workers demonstrated with banners and slogans and there was a small revolution. But thanks to the negotiations of Cañellas and partly to *Montesa's* prestige, the Ministry of Industry contributed some money, in an attempt to save *Ossa* and *Bultaco's* technology and to help *Montesa* reduce its staff from 300 workers to 154. "They could certainly grow again with *Honda*", Cañellas thought. And so it was. Two years after their *Montesa-Honda* venture, they went back to 300 employees thanks to the contribution of technology and product of the Japanese brand. It was an accordion process that was emotionally difficult and that required great adaptation to change from everyone.

Summary – WELLBEING chakra:

Angles	What is assessed?
Emotions	The emotional climate of the workers in the organization.
Adaptability to change	The degree to which our organization adapts to change.
Brand image	Our brand image in the markets we operate.

ORGANIZATIONAL ENERGY SYSTEM (OES)®

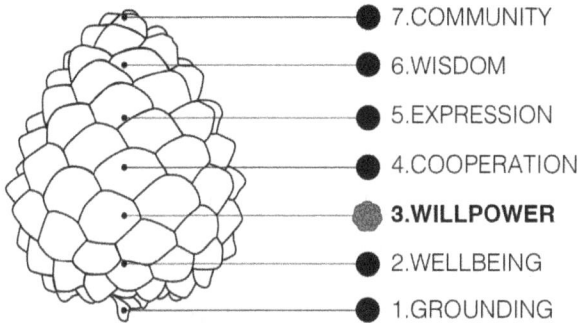

7.COMMUNITY
6.WISDOM
5.EXPRESSION
4.COOPERATION
3.WILLPOWER
2.WELLBEING
1.GROUNDING

Chakra 3: WILLPOWER

The concept in human beings

This chakra is called *Manipura* in Sanskrit, which literally means "bright/shiny gem". Its element is "fire", powerful, energetic and transformative.

In motion, grounded and emotionally flowing, we are now ready to work on our third chakra, related to our will (or willpower). The will is our power and vitality to manifest ourselves, to make our mark in the world to shape or destinies. This energetic center represents our bright gem, understood as our inner energy source. This is where we create our power. Here we transform the power of the first chakra and the flow of the second into the strength necessary for the higher chakras. The third chakra also shelters the human ability for connection and our bonds of union with other human beings. This chakra finds its more powerful expression when it supports the higher energy levels [17].

There are people with an explosive third chakra, while others find it difficult to keep the flame alive. A healthy third chakra is in harmony with the environment, it is warm and subtle. It is not a power developed from control (of oneself or others), but a power that comes from the combination of body and mind, self and others, passion and compassion.

In the human energy system, our power stems from the combination of the upstream and the downstream. The third chakra releases the energy upwards, while the consciousness of the higher chakras descends channeling the energy for a specific purpose. This consciousness, applied to the explosive energy of this chakra (fire) becomes the willpower to act, determination and empowerment. Will is the conscious direction of our energy towards a clear objective. It is the difference between raw energy and real power. To have a strong will, we need to define our goals and our mission.

The existence of desire generates the will to act. Taking control of our lives means taking responsibility for what we do and, consequently, for whatever happens to us. A weak third chakra has no desire or enthusiasm (fire) to fulfill its purpose. When this is the case, people will see themselves as victims of the circumstances with no power to act or impose their own will. A highly developed third chakra will manifest in excessive need for control and power, to mask the real lack of inner strength.

Parallelism in the organization

The interpretation of this chakra in the organizational system leads us to investigate the energy source, the will and determination of an organization. The strength of the people working in an organization should be channeled towards the right purpose, mission and values. Jim Collins in his book "Good to Great" [58] states that for an organization to gain sustainable profitable growth it needs to reconcile its envisioned future through a bold mission statement that represents its core ideology through a set of values.

Furthermore, we need to strike a balance between autonomy of action and control. It will not serve us well to have a great deal of creative energy misdirected (not focused on our mission), or in having a clear purpose but with an excessive degree of control that does not allow our partners for movement and creativity. The mission is also a key organizational tool to connect all partners and establish a virtual link between them. The three angles that define the third organizational chakra are the purpose and mission, the values, and the exercise of power (balance between control and delegation or empowerment).

Purpose and Mission:
First, let us make it clear that these two concepts do not have a single definition. They usually go hand in hand and they are often confused or used interchangeably: the purpose and mission represent the set of fundamental reasons for the existence of the company or organizations. They answer questions like: Who are we? Why are we here? For example, we are a strategic consulting firm in organizational development.

Our mission is to help conscious leaders improve the energy system of their teams and organizations to increase performance and prosperity (economic, social and environmental). Our purpose is to facilitate organizational transformation and personal growth to adapt to the reality of the 21st Century.

The purpose and the mission of a company are usually internal documents. But as long as we do it authentically, we can also share them with customers and the market if we think it can be helpful. Sometimes companies use their mission statement as an advertising slogan, but this is a deviation from its true purpose.

In our work with public and private organizations, it is always surprising to see how poorly developed these two concepts are. If an organization has been operating without a clear purpose and mission for long, it will not be easy to reach consensus on who we are and why we exist. But it is important to do so; otherwise it can become one of the main causes for other organizational symptoms (problems).

All organizations have a clear purpose and mission, at least implicit or unwritten, when they are founded. But it is important to put them on paper. If there are differences regarding the implicit key purpose of the founders, these are likely to surface later and lead to personal conflict. Documenting them accordingly will guarantee that our aims and motivations are the same or, in any case, reconcilable.

In addition, organizations evolve and change owners many times (generational relays, mergers and acquisitions, etc.). With these changes, the unwritten purpose and mission will be more likely to blur and eventually lose their original meaning.

Finally, an unwritten mission and purpose can be confusing and they can be subject to multiple interpretations, especially when the organization has grown significantly. A company with 50,000 workers founded 30 years ago that wants to hire a new employee will need to convey its organizational culture in a clear and consensual manner. And we do not mean here that a couple of well-written paragraphs displayed on the walls will be enough to motivate people. If the mission and purpose are not understood and, more importantly, followed and lived by all, they will not be a guide in their daily actions and decisions.

The mission (and purpose) should also be up-to-date but should not be changed too often. It must adapt to the changing market reality. It is therefore advisable to revise it every few years and assess whether to introduce any changes.

In summary, the first angle of the Willpower chakra assesses whether the purpose and mission of our organization give us strength and guides us in our work.

Purpose and Mission - Examples of good and poor performance

The purpose and mission should be clear and easy to understand. They should not be too long or expressed in technical or complicated language that is unfamiliar to the employees. For example, *Amazon*'s mission is "*to build a place where people can come to find and discover anything they might want to buy online*" [59], whereas *Sony*'s mission could be worded more clearly to have greater force: "*Sony is committed to developing a wide range of innovative products and multimedia services that challenge the way consumers access and enjoy digital entertainment. By ensuring synergy between businesses within the organization, Sony is constantly striving to create exciting new worlds of entertainment that can be experienced on a variety of different products*" [59].

A mission must be specific enough to guide our actions, but also open so as not to limit our development. Take, for example, *Disney*'s mission: "*We create happiness by providing the finest in entertainment for people of all ages, everywhere*" [59]. Any employee can easily relate this mission to what he or she does in the company to improve its performance. Instead, the mission of *Halliburton*, a company that offers a wide range of oilfield services and products for the oil and gas extraction, has too broad a mission: "*To provide real-time solutions to meet our customers' needs*" [59]. This sentence could be the mission for many companies and therefore it is not unique. Something similar happens with *Microsoft*'s mission: "*To help people and businesses throughout the world to realize their full potential*" [59]. Maybe that is what Bill Gates wants to achieve, but there are certainly other ways in which *Microsoft* can help people to realize their full potential, different from a Yoga center, for instance, that could also share the same mission.

The purpose should also be meaningful and inspiring. *CNN* aims to be the company "providing hard-breaking news as it unfolds" [59]. And *Walt Disney* started his theme parks with a clear purpose in mind. He said: "*We are in the business of happiness*" [59]. And we should not underestimate the power of words. Even a small difference can have a significant effect. For example, *Dell Computer*'s mission features the phrase "... *the most successful computer company...*" [59], while *Apple* uses "... *the best personal computing experience...*" [59], and this reflects the kind of "machines" that each of these companies provide to the market. The mission Steve Jobs brought to *Apple* was no doubt one of his greatest contributions, transforming functional yet impersonal machines into *gadgets* people love.

There are missions like *Cara Ellison Corporation's* speak for themselves: "*Get all you can / get away with as much as possible*" [59].

Fortunately, we have increasingly seen young professionals looking for jobs in companies with a purpose and a mission that are meaningful to the world, not just to the company. MBA students are a good example: a sampling conducted a few years ago indicated that many of them wanted a career in jobs with the highest salaries, such as investment banking. Today, more and more young people are starting to gravitate towards more meaningful jobs.

Values:

The issue of values in an organization is also important and closely linked to its mission and purpose. Just like the mission describes who we are and the purpose is the reason why we exist, the corporate values describe how we behave as a collective. In fact, this will only apply to organizations where all the staff has integrated these values. And in most organizations, our organizational values, rather than indicate how we behave, define how we want our people to behave and to operate internally and externally.

As humans, we have a personal belief system that defines our individual values. Organizations also have a belief system built from their foundation and that has developed over time. These beliefs, as we will discuss in more detail in the seventh chakra, determine the values that prevail in the body. A small company with its founder or founders alive will have certain values, written or unwritten, in accordance with that original belief system; whereas a large company that has existed for two or more generations, and/or that has undergone major changes, may need to consciously remember and promote these values we identify or want to be identified with.

It is clear that all individuals bring their own values to work. The challenge for organizations is to make each of these individuals share their core values. If one of our values is transparency and one of our employees finds it very difficult to act accordingly, our organizational development process will strive to help that person to eventually overcome this difficulty, which might be cultural.

Therefore, corporate values are a finite list of values (from 3 to 7, for example) that an organization decides to share with their colleagues and with the world. And that list needs to be explained and defined, a word is not enough. For instance, if we choose the value of honesty, it would be of great help to define exactly what that organization understands it is. Thus, our potential for organizational development necessarily implies recognizing that we may not be all embracing the same values and that we have to promote them among our colleagues gradually. And nothing works better than the owners and the managers leading by example and becoming role-models.

This list of values can also have a priority order so as to guide our daily work more clearly. *Disney* theme parks have four values in order of priority: safety, courtesy, entertainment and efficiency. So if, for example, an employee hears someone shouting nearby while he is politely helping a customer, he will know exactly how he is supposed to react.

In summary, the second angle of the Willpower chakra assesses whether corporate values are shared and if there is a consistency with the actions.

Values - Examples of good and poor performance

We have all seen organizations where the desired values are just an intellectual exercise at an off-site or where they were chosen from a long list of nice words. Most certainly, these are far from representing our behavior in the company. If the organization owners, managers and executives are not able to adopt the values themselves and lead by example, it is best not to even mention them. Corporate values, together with our mission and purpose, define our corporate culture as they influence our collective and individual behaviors. You can change corporate culture, as you can change the beliefs of a person, but it takes time and effort. From management positions, we can only work to promote values that are not present in the organization if we are determined and prepared to invest time and resources. Publishing a list of corporate values that are not fulfilled will have a more negative effect than just not addressing the issue of values at all.

One of the corporate values of a company we once worked for was *"People first / respect for people"*. And it was true for many years. It was a nice place to work where employees could feel respected. They were more than just a number and there was a strong psychological contract between employees and managers. The company grew while suffering the pressures of a low-margin market. At one point, many of the workers and even executives started to put down the poster that had proudly displayed their values for years. They argued: "*I cannot pretend to promote the values that the owners and managers are not able to comply with; on many occasions, I am forced to make decisions that are not in line with those values. Either that or leave the company...*" And of course, leaving the company is not easy. But the question we need to ask ourselves here is: how bridging our own values is affecting the climate, motivation and psychological contract in the organization? And what about performance?

Another interesting example is a 'national' effort to define societal values in order to face the challenges of the 21st Century. The importance of values as forces that organize and give sense to a collective, even an entire society, has been well understood by the Government of Catalonia. We know this case well because since 2010 Pinea3 has been actively collaborating in the development of the *National Plan of Values of Catalonia*. This is a one of a kind initiative, promoted and independent diagnose of the "best" values lived and exemplified in such region of Spain. A wide array of representatives of the civil society, organized around 21 different areas (e.g. health, education, organizations, etc.), met regularly and proposed a number of strategic lines. The Government embraced these lines and transformed them into programs and actions that would promote such 'new paradigm values' in Catalonia. Our contribution in the area of organizations put light into developing and managing organizations with a bigger sense, more humane and systemic.

Power:

The third angle of the third organizational chakra has to do with the exercise of power. Power may be exercised to any degree in the continuum from dictatorship (on one end) to anarchy (on the other). Most likely, the suitable point is neither end but a happy medium. But where exactly? Each organization will need to define the right balance. The most appropriate may not be the same for a nuclear power plant, a police force, a video game start-up or an architecture firm. Steve Jobs, for example, was a manager who paid great attention to detail, what many considered excessive micro-management. But his obsession with product design and aesthetics led *Apple* to launch stylish user-friendly products that have captured the market.

Having said this, employers have always erred on the side of too much control, influenced by the historical division between the bourgeoisie and the proletariat, and acting from the belief that people do not work unless there is control. This control finds its natural environment in countries with strong pyramidal hierarchies like Russia, Singapore, France and Spain to a lesser extent.

Modern organizations following the new paradigm have been talking for decades about delegation and empowerment; not only to update an old-fashioned system of beliefs, but also because it is more profitable financially. An organization that delegates decisions downwards and empowers the employee is an organization that relies on people and allows them to take responsibility for their job. This has several advantages. First, it creates spaces for owners and managers to deal with more strategic issues so that they do not have to run here and there putting out fires. Moreover, it motivates collaborators, who feel useful and can develop their creative capacity, finding solutions suited to their reality.

A corporate culture promoting responsibility and empowerment will have project leaders and team members rather than managers, and subordinates. There will be reliable self-managed teams rather than administration and enforcement teams. Ken Blanchard proposes three keys to empowerment: *"sharing information, establishing boundaries and replacing the old hierarchy with self-managed teams and individuals"* [60].

In summary, the third angle of the Willpower chakra assesses how power is exercised (control vs. delegation) and whether there is autonomy of action.

Power - Examples of good and poor performance

Consider the case of a fire department or an army. It is clear that once the general strategy and guidelines are established, these groups should have flexibility of action when they are doing their field work. Just as these mobile units will need to adapt to the present situation, teams in an organization will also work better if they have the ability to decide how to reach their goal.

Now imagine a football team. There should be some basic rules as for who does what, where each one should move, the opponent being marked, etc. But the collective creativity in the field is a key determinant for success. Similarly, a profit-making company will work better if employees are always empowered to decide what to do at an operational level. For example, the *Marriott* hotel chain gives the employees who are serving customers a small budget. When necessary, they have the freedom to make decisions that improve customer satisfaction. A customer in a hurry once left his suitcase at reception and called from the airport to report it. As the receptionist did not have to consult with anyone else, she could make the decision to send the suitcase with an urgent courier paid by the hotel. A company that limits operational decisions to its managers may end up disappointing many customers. *Call-center* services are an example of this. Sometimes it is like talking to a machine. Of course the individuals who work there are not to blame, but the design of the system should be revised.

Google, the company we have mentioned in many of the examples, has a work philosophy based on empowerment and confidence in individuals. *Whole Foods*, a supermarket chain of quality products, is also a business community known for its empowerment to all the teams managing their supermarkets. *Gore-Tex* is another good example for being a non-hierarchical company based on self-managed teams. *IKEA* has also created a highly decentralized environment and is a model of flat structure that has kept its core values like honesty, simplicity, humility and diversity alive.

Small and medium entrepreneurs often say, "Delegate? I wish! But my people are not prepared and I have too much work to train them, it is just not realistic". This manager may be right about the resources available, but what is the problem with this position? Who does the solution to the problem depend on? It is like saying "I have no time to prevent fires because I am putting them out all day." Or else: "Of course health always comes first, but I have no time to go to the gym". Either we manage to spend part of our time being proactive or anticipating the future, or the whirlwind of reality will inevitably absorb us. In their book *The Leadership Pipeline* [61] Charan, Drotter and Noel describe the typical mistakes people make when they are promoted to the next level of the corporate ladder. Being promoted usually comes through doing our work very well on the lower level for instance, so the inertia is to continue doing what made us successful in the past instead of delegating to the team.

Willpower Chakra – The COOB '92 Case:

Let us see the case of COOB '92 (Barcelona Olympic Organizing Committee '92), an excellent case to illustrate an organization with a strong Willpower.

> Note that the element of this chakra is fire, the source of power, the drive and the determination of an organization. The Olympic Games, held in different cities every four years, mobilize a large number of people who gather around a common project to make this event a reality. These companies, despite being short-term, must function effectively for the

games to run smoothly and safely welcome thousands of visitors from around the world.

The '92 Barcelona Olympics were, and still are for many, a role-model to follow. Not only because of the good organization, but also for what is known as the post-Olympics effect, what the organization leaves to the city and the territory. In this case, Barcelona opened to the world and improved a series of basic infrastructures for the city: the beach was re-covered, the ring road surrounding the city was built, the airport expanded and the suburbs restructured. It also gained the 'Villa Olímpica', the Olympic village, and other facilities currently used for social purposes.

The organization itself is not unimportant. Staging the Olympic Games is a macro-project that requires coordination at multiple levels: political, security, infrastructure, communication, sports and customer service. In addition, the deadlines are strict and there is great pressure because the event has high international visibility. It is therefore one of the most important events for the local community and across the country. The COOB '92 mobilized 1,100 professionals during four years, 5,000 people on temporary contracts in the last year of preparation, and about 100,000 volunteers to meet a variety of needs during the course of the games (image and sound technicians, drivers, security, transla-tors, public relations, etc.).

We have chosen this organization as a good example of willpower. The implicit force and motivation that led this project should be the envy of most companies. Joan Rafel, responsible for recruitment and train-ing of the COOB '92, recalled: "*I do not remember any other group of people in any organization with a clearer sense of purpose and mission. These would give strength to the work of all employees every day.*" Their mission and purpose were not written and published, but they were im-plicitly so clear that no one questioned them. The organization of these games was the chance for Barcelona and for Spain to prove that they were worthy of belonging to the 'European club'. Note that Spain joined the former European Economic Community (EEC), today EU, in 1986. The country wanted to prove that they could live up to the expectations; not only receiving tourists on the beaches, but also organizing perhaps the most important international event that would put them in the spot-light for a while. The purpose was so strong that it brought together political groups, public and private institutions. They put their differences aside and worked together towards a greater common purpose. It was a time to transcend, as individuals, as a city and as a country.

Jordi Olivé, who worked as sound technician in the six months be-fore the games, lived the experience similarly: "*I remember the strength we received from having a clear direction and a common goal, it really brought us together*". "*Companies should always seek to have a mission and a purpose that are clear and shared*", says Olivé.

Values also played an important role in the success of the event. Once again, these were not written, but they were lived and practiced everyday: proximity, collaboration, quality and (most importantly) fun. *"There was a festive, enthusiastic atmosphere"*, says Rafel. Another value that was strongly present in the organization of the games was delegation, which was equally important to spread that fire, the central energy, the motivation, the willingness of the organization and all its employees. The COOB '92 had little hierarchy. Instead, there was decentralization and empowerment, for reasons related with the design of the games or out of real need.

Everyone who worked there had such good memories that when the games were over and the organization dissolved, Joan Rafel looked for an occupation that would be as challenging and worthy. He worked for *Médecins Sans Frontières as* HR manager for a few years. In 2012, Joan was the Corporate Director of People and Organization at *Abertis*. *"It is the mission itself that empowers people and we could spoil it, because people are naturally motivated. So we have to manage not to discourage them. Taking the mission of the company seriously is very important for any organization"*, says Rafel.

Summary – WILLPOWER chakra:

Angles	What is assessed?
Purpose and Mission	Whether the purpose and mission of our organization give us strength and guide us in our work.
Values	Whether the corporate values are shared and there is consistency with the actions.
Power	How power is exercised (control vs. delegation) and whether there is autonomy of action.

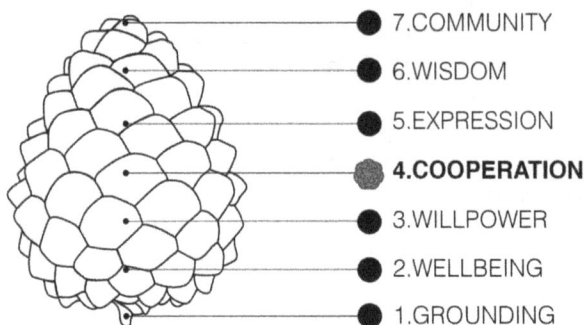

7.COMMUNITY
6.WISDOM
5.EXPRESSION
4.COOPERATION
3.WILLPOWER
2.WELLBEING
1.GROUNDING

Chakra 4: COOPERATION

The concept in human beings

This chakra is called *Anahata* in Sanskrit, literally meaning "non-collision (the sound which comes without the striking of any two things together)". Its element is "air", light and harmonious, which expands and fills all the space that contains it.

The fourth chakra is in the center of the human energy system. It simultaneously divides and unites the lower and the higher chakras: it is the ceiling of the lower chakras (body and matter) and the root of the higher (mind and spirit). It is known as the heart chakra for being located in this area of the body.

This chakra is the center of love, compassion, peace and harmony. Powered by the passion and will of the third chakra, it has a motivating energy that radiates and spreads to everything in its path. Universal love is the ability to establish appropriate and meaningful relationships with our environment and to experience compassion and connection with everything around us. If our willpower has done its job, we will be in the "right place", in our center. Then we can relax, accept, allow, be open and receive. We will operate from a status of trust and balance.

The fourth chakra is governed by the principle of balance. Striking a healthy balance with ourselves, our relationships and the environment will help us achieve a state of serenity and peace. Without that balance, relationships (internal or external) will crumble. 'The sound which comes without the striking of any two things together' comes

Organizational Energy System (OES)®

from a voluntary exchange of energy, both from the giver and the receiver. Commitment comes from a balance of the needs, desires and challenges. This relational balance includes the relationship between the lower chakras (matter) and the higher (spirit), the balance between love for oneself and love for others, the balance between giving and receiving.

If the fourth chakra is closed, there will be a tendency to introspection and even a fear of interpersonal relationships. When this chakra is blocked, the whole energy system is suppressed and it will be difficult for the energy to circulate upwards. There might be a disconnection between body and mind. If this chakra is excessively open, we tend to give too much and we live our lives through others rather than operate from our center.

In summary, the mission of the fourth chakra is to achieve a state of balance with ourselves and with our external relationships, from love and compassion.

Parallelism in the organization

The interpretation of this chakra has to do with the relational balance inside and outside the organization. Since the word Love is still somehow taboo in the business world, this relational balance can be understood as the degree and quality of internal and external cooperation. The quality of this cooperation will increase if there is balance, compassion, trust and, ultimately, if there is love (understood here as a universal concept). Respect for individual differences (valuing diversity), which we saw in the angle of *Emotions* (second chakra) it is also present here and undoubtedly will enhance or hinder true cooperation.

There are five relational acts that can also help us understand this chakra in an organizational or executive environment: ask, offer, receive, agree and acknowledge. Depending on how you carry out these relational acts, there will be more or less harmony and balance in relationships and cooperation (inside and outside the organization).

The three angles we chose to define the fourth organizational chakra are cooperation with external entities (partners, intermediaries, suppliers…), internal cooperation and customer relationship.

Cooperation with external entities:
The first angle of the fourth organizational chakra refers to the cooperation with partners outside the company and the environment of the organization in general except for our customers (that we address sepa-

rately with its own angle). Depending on the market where we operate, the different players: suppliers, distributors, strategic partners and even competitors, will be more or less relevant.

Honest collaboration with our suppliers is relatively recent in the West. It was possible thanks to the success in the 70s and 80s of Japanese companies like *Sony* and *Toyota* that popularized a more global view of the system and a fair treatment of suppliers. In many cultures and sectors (like automotive), suppliers had been improperly treated for decades.

Distributors outside the company are often underestimated and undervalued, especially if our company has a very strong name and brand image. But companies that have been able to take care of these relationships, keeping a fair, balanced cooperation with their distributors or retailers are the most successful businesses today. In order to reduce the funding needed to grow globally, many companies have opted for franchises. Are these external or internal to the company? How do we cooperate with them?

Strategic partners are perhaps the only category of external entities that has received special attention and care. As the name suggests, our business depends on these agreements to some extent. But this does not mean that such relationships have always been approached from honesty, let alone from love and compassion.

Finally, cooperation with competitors is increasingly common. In fact, the word "coopetition" is already used to refer to those relationships in between cooperation and competition. In the next section we will illustrate these concepts with a few examples.

In summary, the first angle of the Cooperation chakra assesses the degree of cooperation with our business environment (external partners, suppliers, competitors) and whether this is done for the common good.

Cooperation with external entities - Examples of good and poor performance

Cooperation with an external entity does not necessarily mean signing a written or formal agreement. It actually refers to how we collaborate with them. We need to analyze to what extent this cooperation is forced or it is honest cooperation seeking the famous *win-win*. There are examples of successful cooperation at all levels. An example of cooperation between competitors is *HP* laser printers. All the central mechanisms that move the paper in these printers are based on *Canon's* patents. At one point in their history, the senior managers of the two companies met to discuss the possibility of a *win-win* deal for both. *HP*, with most of the market share worldwide, would benefit from a more advanced mechanism rather than have to develop its own, avoiding *Canon* patents. And *Canon*, also selling laser printers and competing with *HP*, would benefit from the volume of its competitor, as they would receive a small percentage for every printer sold. This agreement has been successful for many years thanks to the spirit of cooperation from both sides.

We could also think of many other co-opetition examples like: Apple and Microsoft building closer ties on software development; Sony and Phillips jointly setting the new standards for DVD players. The free open source Linux and the Android standards are also very good examples of global scale collaboration across many entities and sectors.

We can see many other types of cooperation in the markets. The important thing here is to assess, formally or informally, the degree of cooperation and if it is honest and done for the common good. Some could wonder: "And so what if it is not honest, or not for the good of both? I am a very good negotiator and I can take advantage". The same happens in a personal relationship with our partner, a relative or a friend. Such relationships will never last, if they are not honest or there is no balance in giving-receiving and in risk-opportunity. In consequence, they will not stand the test of time and we will have to re-invest in another relationship. Furthermore, if an organization does not seek external cooperation for the common good, they will not be able to cooperate internally either. And this is negative energy that will eventually turn against itself.

We can all think of examples of organizations that successfully collaborate externally with a *win-win* attitude. Consider cases like the Japanese companies we mentioned before. Or *Apple,* for example, who have created a collaboration model around the *AppStore*, and *Procter & Gamble,* who collaborate with external designers for R&D functions traditionally developed at home through their *Connect & Develop* program.

There are millions of other examples and not all are profit-making companies. In October 2011, local businessmen in a small town outside Barcelona decided to donate money to finish the works for some town facilities that the Town Hall had started but did not have the funds to finish.

Similarly, we all have examples of organizations that have failed or have not wanted to cooperate honestly or for the common good.

Internal cooperation:

The second angle of this chakra relates to internal cooperation between individuals, departments, divisions, across business units or countries. Competition is healthy and natural if you are looking for personal growth and achievement. But it becomes a problem if it seeks the collapse and failure of the other. It is a fine line where many of us have been and it is important to understand that, when taken to the wrong place, it is a very negative energy for the organization.

In this section, words are unnecessary. We all know when we are co-operating honestly and for the good of both and when we are not. We know it because our heart can tell us immediately. How many fiefdoms have we seen in organizations we have worked for? And where the aim was the personal benefit rather than the common good? And how would the same organization operate if we could inspire some spirit of collabo-ration and love? Winning organizations are and will be, those that foster a true spirit of internal cooperation.

When there is genuine cooperation between our employees, we can develop a higher sense of trust in the organization. This will be part of the corporate culture. Trust is a catalyst for conflict resolution, for group cohesion and for the development of team creativity and for overall busi-ness performance. Here we see the influence of cooperation in creative and innovative processes.

In summary, the second angle of the Cooperation chakra assesses in-ternal cooperation and the degree of trust among our employees.

Internal Cooperation - Examples of good and poor performance

An example of an organization recognized for its high level of inter-nal collaboration is *FC Barcelona* team during the years that coach Pep Guardiola was in charge. The cooperation model between the coach and the players and between the players themselves on the field has become a world class referent. It has been acclaimed as the best soccer team by many experts, thanks to a very different game and collaboration strategy where individuality was not as much appreciated as teamwork. Think how we could apply the same concept to our company.

An example of poor internal collaboration that was front page on the sports news for a while was the NBA delay to start the American basket-ball league. From the scheduled start, November 1st 2011, it was delayed until Christmas Day. The tense negotiations between the NBA owners and the players blocked the labor agreement for weeks and they had to

Organizational Energy System (OES)®

cancel the pre-season and several weeks of the season. According to the commissioner of the league, it was not profitable for most of the 30 NBA owners, who had lost a total of 300 million dollars in the 2010-11 season. The average player salary was approximately 5 million dollars and they not only refused to reduce it but they demanded 7 million instead. There were players who just wanted to play and opposed blocking the negotiations, but the players' union controlled the negotiations of the collective agreement. It is clear that individual interests, possibly on both sides, led the NBA to call off 14 of the 82 regular games in the 2011-2012 season.

An example of confidence in the business world is *Facebook*. In early 2009 the leaders of the company announced a change in the conditions of use: *Facebook* could make unrestricted use of everything posted by its users. Following the announcement, the U.S. blog *The Consumerist* strongly protested against this change of policy in personal information privacy. Thousands of users joined the protest because the company's initiative was a breach of trust to the social network. The movement against this announcement was such that *Facebook* founder Mark Zuckerberg had to ensure that people will continue to own their information and control who they share it with.

We have chosen a few examples that have captured the public attention, but we all know of many examples, also current ones, in our close environment. Internal cooperation is one of the clearest angles of the Organizational Energy System (OES) with the greatest significance on business results. We can only improve it if we do it authentically, from the heart. But this might not be an easy task, because there are many egos we have to fight, starting with our own.

Customer relationship:
The third angle of the fourth chakra specifically refers to the relationship with our customers. How do we cooperate with them? What is the degree of customer service? Do we really care for them or do we just want their money?

Successful organizations positively know that everything begins and ends with the customer. This implies a radical change in the behavior and attitude of our employees and leaders. It also entails moving away from viewing customers only as the receiving end of the chain. Customer-focused companies, like the *Marriott* Hotel chain we discussed earlier, are gradually winning customers; whereas organizations focused on their own good rather than the customer's, end up being set aside when the user has a choice.

Sometimes it is not even clear who the customer is. Absurd as it seems at first sight, it is not. Let us review a couple of examples: the first is that of a risk prevention company. Who is the end customer? The company to whom we provide the service to, the one that pays for the invoices, or the employee of that company, who we want to prevent from damage? The answers will have implications as for how we organize and which customer we intend to satisfy. Another example is that of a company with independent franchisees. Who is the end customer? The franchisee or the user of the service or final product? Who do we want to provide service? From a pure economic view, we tend to satisfy the one that pays our invoices. If we act like this and we lose the balance between the three 'P's (people, planet, profit) for too long, our prosperity will decrease and we will develop energy blockages, organizational diseases that could endanger our long-term existence.

In summary, the third angle of the Cooperation chakra assesses whether there is a good relationship with our customers.

Customer relationship - Examples of good and poor performance
At the risk of using a cliché, there is the example of mobile phone operators. It seems that all these companies care for is our contract and that there is only real customer service when our continuity with them is threatened. Wouldn't we like a company where we could feel confident that they are doing their best for us?

Many companies have realized that if customer service is honest, the return will be priceless; even if we think we are investing too much time on it in the short-term. In the 70s, when the trend was to adopt the self-service system, *Domo Gas*, a chain of gas service stations in Western Canada, understood that people wanted to get in and out of the station as quickly as possible. So they designed a gas service station inspired by the pit stops of car races. When a customer arrived, two or three employees rushed to serve him, fill up with fuel, clean the windscreen and check the water conducts under the hood. Californian fast-food chain *In-N-Out Burger* has also become very successful serving quality burgers with a fast and excellent service.

Cooperation Chakra - The AFANOC / La Casa dels Xuklis case:
Let us now look at the *AFANOC* association, a case that will allow us to explore the cooperation chakra and its three angles.

We will analyze the case of *AFANOC* (Association of Relatives and Friends of Oncology Children of Catalonia), a very good example to discuss cooperation in the new paradigm, especially with their project *La Casa dels Xuklis*. Since it is not a well-known organization, we will briefly explain its origins and evolution.

AFANOC was set up by a group of parents to children with cancer in 1987, with the aim of improving their quality of life. At that time the survival rate for these cases in Spain was 50%. They realized it was partly due to the lack of resources and low awareness of the problem (it was an isolating disease with ongoing ancestral taboos and the resources available were not suited for children or long-term illnesses). This association is an example of co-operation, though it has not always been a bed of roses. They began as a support group for people with the same problems, fears, joys and sorrows, but they soon realized that it was not enough. Then they started a period of vindication that was sometimes hard, with all the players involved in the process. They learned to negotiate and to work together in order to find a balance between giving and receiving. The support group asked for basic things like being able to stay in the hospital with their children 24 hours a day. The next stage came when they realized that if they wanted things to be done faster, they had to do them on their own. So they decided to manage the Association according to business criteria, where the profit would be a social benefit. They professionalized the association's team and launched a series of funding projects and improvement initiatives such as having volunteers on the children's oncology floor at Hospital Vall d'Hebron, one of the reference hospitals in Barcelona treating child cancer. Once the basic needs were covered, *AFANOC* entered its fourth and current stage, where the association works with all the parties involved (government, private companies, hospitals, professionals and other entities). "It is a period of consensus where we build on the basis of non-confrontation", explained Josep Pla, one of the founders and President of the association. *AFANOC* carries out activities inside hospitals (like craft workshops and story-telling) and outside (through education on the disease, psychological support to families and aid for re-insertion) together with a group of 363 volunteers. The team works horizontally and it is an excellent example of internal cooperation based on trust, where motivation for work does not only come from financial reward.

In 2008, 1,350 children and teenagers were being diagnosed with cancer in Spain .Since treatments lasted for months and sometimes for several years, there were around 6,000 children being treated in Spain in 2008. More than 25% went to Barcelona to receive the treatment. The 40% of these families that came from outside the city did not have a place to stay or money to pay for a hotel. Many relatives had to leave their jobs to be with their children and many others, as there were no alternatives, had yet another problem finding accommodation.

The same year, the Provincial Council of Barcelona donated a plot of 3,660 square meters (next to the Hospital Vall d'Hebron) to the association. They would build a shelter home for patients and relatives from outside the city with no economic means. This would be their place to stay in Barcelona during their children's treatment: *La Casa dels Xuklis* (*Xuklis' Place*). The *Xuklis* are fictional characters who live in the neighboring park of Collserola and feed on the pain and suffering of the people. The *Xuklis* slurp ("*xuclen*" in Catalan) the sadness, pain and bad energy and they are invisible for the grown-ups. This residence can accommodate up to 25 families in apartments designed and built as a true example of external collaboration. It was designed by the architecture firm MBM (Martorell-Bohigas-Mackay) and many suppliers collaborated voluntarily. More than 30 designers decorated the apartments completely for free, all of them different and absolutely fascinating (see: http://www.lacasadelsxuklis.org/). Many of the professionals left saying: "Thanks for letting me work for free".

Certainly, *AFANOC* and *La Casa dels Xuklis* are also an example of "customer" relationship. The stay in this residence is completely free, "the house is yours", they welcome their guests. And when they return to their home towns, they keep in touch with the association in an active way.

Today 80% of the children with cancer are cured. The *AFANOC* association and *La Casa dels Xuklis* have won many awards. They have become a referent highlighting the importance of psychological and social impact on treatments. *La Casa dels Xuklis* is a shelter home determined to become a European psycho-social benchmark in the fight against cancer.

Summary – COOPERATION chakra:

Angles	What is assessed?
Cooperation with external entities	The degree of cooperation with our business environment (external partners, suppliers, competitors) and if it is done for the common good.
Internal cooperation	Internal cooperation and the degree of trust among our employees.
Customer relationship	The quality of the relationship with our customers (attention, cooperation).

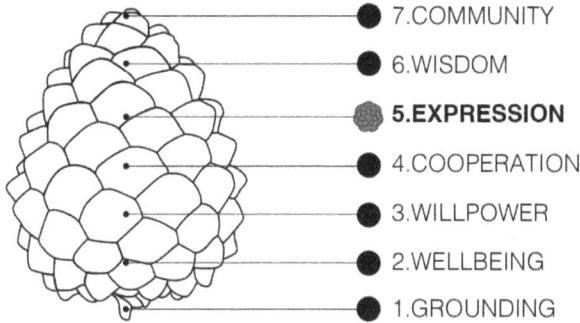

- 7.COMMUNITY
- 6.WISDOM
- **5.EXPRESSION**
- 4.COOPERATION
- 3.WILLPOWER
- 2.WELLBEING
- 1.GROUNDING

Chakra 5: EXPRESSION

The concept in human beings

This chakra is called *Vissudha* in Sanskrit, which literally means "puri-fication". Its element is "sound", one of the most important forms of expression and creativity in humans.

Sound is the rhythmic vibration of air molecules. When we enter the fifth chakra, we experience the world in the form of vibrations. These vibrations are thinner as we move up in the human energy system. So this chakra helps us purify by refining the most physical vibrations of the lower chakras. In doing so, our communication will be clearer and more harmonious with the environment.

When these vibrations produce a state of harmony between them, there is a deep sense of connection and expansion, and we can enter a state of internal resonance. When we communicate with others, this state of harmony is also noticeable by those who are, so to speak, in line with us. This means that someone's comments will add value to someone else's, instead of going against each other. Two people who are in har-mony could say the same thing at the same time. For example, musicians know that a band can only play well if they keep the rhythm of the piece they are playing. On the other hand, if there is no harmony between two people, communication will be inefficient and each party will under-stand whatever they want to.

Improving this energetic center requires a deep commitment with the truth, as well as expressing ourselves with integrity. When this center is healthy, a power emerges and directs our vital force towards creativity and self-expression.

The fifth chakra is the nexus between the physical and the metaphysical world (the world of ideas). This chakra will be healthy when we are internally unified and externally expanded. Then true creativity can emerge. A fifth chakra developed in excess might lead to over communicating without saying much. If this chakra is deficient, there will be difficulties in communication. A lack of self-esteem or self-confidence, or just a poor sense of grounding, can cause the fifth chakra to block.

Parallelism in the organization

The parallelism of this chakra in the organizational energy system has to do with our expression, our rhythm and our resonance as a group, both internally and externally.

Just like a choir who cannot sing in tune unless they follow the rhythm, the members of our organization cannot express themselves harmoniously if there is no resonance within the group and each one is expressing their organizational truth in a different way.

To improve external and internal communication in our organization, we need to refine our vibrational energy. This energy will be better if people at work really listen to each other and vibrate with one another (if there is a deep connection between collaborators and employees).

We will work on the three angles of this organizational chakra: external communication of the company or organization, internal upward and horizontal communication, and internal downward communication.

External communication:
The organizational external communication is related to all those forms of external expression, including all our traditional actions in marketing, communication and public relations. But it also includes more subtle and up-to-date forms of external communication. For example, the actions and discourse of our sales people, the role of a middle manager invited to participate in a round table, or dealing with external complaints via phone, letter, email or *twitter*. The number of external communications of all types will eventually define our image in the market, so it is important to have a complete view of our external communication.

With the existence of the Internet, external communication nowadays seems to be everything that is said on the net, by our partners or not, and it seems to be running through our fingers. In their book "*La Reconciliación con el consumidor*" [62] ('The Reconciliation with the Consumer'), Virgili and Wallovits claim that companies no longer write their history on their own. The authors argue that the brand image not only depends on the organization and its corporate communication, but on customers and users. If 100 million people agree on the Internet that *Coca-Cola* should change their packaging, for instance, the company will have to do it if they want to keep them as customers. In fact, this already happened with the famous "*Green my Apple*", a play on words meaning 'make computers greener'. With this motto, *Apple* users promoted a campaign to ask Steve Jobs to adopt a more sustainable attitude with their products. The company had to do it and, seen in perspective, it was actually a very successful move for the brand. We will explain below the more recent case of *Gap*, the fashion retail chain.

The external communication of an organization must be honest and consistent with their values in order to have strength. We agree with O'Toole and Warren who state that "no organization can be honest with the public if it's not honest with itself" [15]. A good question to consider regarding this angle is: how many lies do we have to tell to sell our products or services? Only companies that express their inner-truth will endure.

In summary, the first angle of the Expression chakra assesses the external communication of our organization.

External communication - Examples of good and poor performance

Many companies are famous in the market for their excellent external communication through clever positioning. Remember the "*Just do it*" by *Nike* or the "*Intel Inside*" by *Microsoft*.

An example of a company with a good external communication is *Timberland*. They have created a 'world of love and enjoyment of nature' and express this essence consistently and coherently, using a very wide range of media. Their logo, for instance, connects with the archetypal tree representing a life in harmony with nature. Their on- and off-line advertising conveys the image of a company with a genuine interest in nature and outdoor lifestyle. It is part of their corporate culture and that translates into a feeling of authenticity for anyone in contact with the brand. In addition, the company has developed an image of expertise in organic materials, also making it a good option for those who want to buy eco-friendly. They have videos on how the clothes are made, how to optimize the use of materials or how these can be recycled. Therefore, *Timberland* proved through all their actions that they are aligned with a vision of harmonious outdoor life.

Here is an example of the strength of the 2.0 market in relation to a company's external communication. In October 2010 *Gap* unveiled a new logo in an attempt to renew their image. But the public reaction was quick and decisive. Through the social networks a large number of customers said they did not like the new brand image. The company's management grasped the message and discarded the new logo in a swift reaction. They also saw it as a great opportunity to interact with consumers and they decided to set up a contest. *Gap* fans could submit a new logo design and the best proposal would become the new brand image. Once again, the public turned out to be smarter than a bunch of marketing experts. Social networks made it clear that people did not like the promotional approach that the company had taken. A *twitter* account specifically created to display the new *Gap* logo received some offensive remarks about their history. Fans also published many negative messages on *Gap*'s *Facebook* page. In just six days, the company had to go back to their old logo, clearly approved by their consumers.

Internal upward (bottom-up) and horizontal communication:
Internal communication is one of the pending issues of many organizations that send information downwards but neglect to hear the feedback or to establish effective communication channels across the organization.

In an open corporate culture where you can go talk to a more senior person easily, bottom-up communication will be better than in a company where there is an atmosphere of fear or with a very strong hierarchy. The more fluent this upward communication is, the better the organization leaders will understand the business reality. Therefore, we must listen and be willing to listen, which is usually easier said than done.

Egos, time pressure or the pursuit of efficiency can be the enemies of complete and thorough listening. Many times while we are listening, we are busy thinking of an answer, judging, or just thinking about our stuff.

Thinking that managers should know all the answers and subordinates execute the orders is simply outdated. There is widespread evidence that a creative company allows their employees to contribute the best of themselves. This implies creating spaces and processes so that the information flows upwards as well as horizontally.

If the information does not flow smoothly, it can eventually result in "pending" conversations that can become business cancers. They are like "dead elephants" in a room that we can all see but nobody talks about. Everyone just turns around and "walks by", contributing to the known effect of "groupthink".

O'Toole and Bennis published an article on Harvard Business Review (HBR) [15] where they explain and justify how a culture of candor (that which communicates honestly and transparently) improves its performance. They refer to all communications, upward, horizontal and downward but make a special emphasis on creating a culture of trust and dialogue, where disagreeing and challenging the own assumptions is priced.

In summary, the second angle of the Expression chakra assesses the effectiveness of bottom-up and horizontal communication within the company.

Internal upward and horizontal communication - Examples of good and poor performance

This angle is closely related to the internal cooperation angle we saw in the fourth chakra. There cannot be cooperation unless there is a good horizontal communication. Most up-to-date large companies have learned the lesson and have communication policies that encourage and promote communication and *cross-fertilization* between departments, geographies, projects and business units. In practice, these policies and processes will have a varying degree of success depending on the egos of the individuals they come across.

There are companies that still have not made the transition to the new paradigm in key factors like communication, one of the foundations of everything else. In the past we collaborated with a company that was interested in our work to reconcile two opposing sides within the management board. There had been a recent change of the CEO and, as usual in these cases, the incoming person established policies and lines of action that were very different from those of the previous CEO. That was how the members of the board of directors were divided between those who supported the previous line of action and those aligned with the new CEO. Moreover, the company was a very conservative organization. There had not been much movement of staff over the years, which favored the creation of hermetic departments and divisions operating independently of each other. Our job was to soften these differences and promote better horizontal communication. Bottom-up communication had also been influenced by the hierarchical control structure governing the company. As a result, pending conversations accumulated between certain individuals and as a group in general.

As we will see in the following sections, an organization with poor internal communication is likely to have other problems in their energy system, like a vision, mission and values that are not shared or clear, as well as poor decision-making that can prevent progress.

Google is an example of a company where a great deal is invested to ensure there is good communication at all levels. They have an open-door policy where employees can approach any manager to discuss the problems they might have, even if they are encouraged to do it first with their direct manager. Besides, they have successfully implemented the classical suggestion box and something much more innovative they call *whiteboard culture*. There are large whiteboards throughout the company where employees can start or add ideas on any topic, from new products to "daily life" at *Google*.

In addition, *Google* understands that not everyone feels comfortable speaking in public, so they regularly undertake surveys to ask employees for feedback on several topics anonymously. And, most importantly, there is a follow-up on these surveys. They develop or improve existing plans based on the results, post them on their Intranet and ask the managers to discuss them with their teams.

Google also promotes cross-functional communication through a blogging tool for internal use. All employees can start their own blog, post their progress on current assignments, or share notes about a project or personal stories.

There are other organizations and companies which constitute a historical example of good practices in communication (e.g. Honeywell, Continental Airlines, Johnson & Johnson, Nordstrom, Whole Foods, Xilinx and DaVita). The CEO of DaVita, for instance, a dialysis treatment operator, has the policy of "no secrets" to foster trust across all stakeholders. He actively seeks "the bad news" and rewards who give it to him as it is a learning opportunity to avoid future mistakes [15].

Internal downward (top-down) communication:
This is the kind of internal communication we usually pay more attention to. How do we communicate with all our employees? This is certainly the first step and a very important one. What are our communication channels downwards? Email, memoranda, processes and informal

chats among others. Here we are not only talking about top-down communication from managers, but about how the messages from executives and middle managers are transmitted to each of their employees.

The first question to consider is: who decides whether communication is good or poor, the sender or the receiver? Many of us immediately tend to complain about our receiver for not understanding what we have said. If someone does not understand us, it means we have failed to communicate with him or her. There is a problem in the transmission of information, not necessarily solved by repeating the same but louder and sounder. Perhaps the communication channel is not suitable for that person or group, or maybe there is "noise" in the communication (because of the language, for instance), or just an excess of information clouding clear communication. But it is always the receiver who decides whether communication is good or poor.

And even when the receiver gets our message, the interpretation of our words can be different from the intention we had in mind. This happens because a person might have mental patterns (individual or cultural) different from ours. Hence, we see that effective communication requires a bi-directional approach, partly represented by the bottom-up communication we saw in the previous angle.

Effective communication involves much more than just saying something or sending an email. Communication is a complex process and therefore it can be improved in most organizations.

In summary, the third angle of the Expression chakra assesses top-down communication within the company.

Internal downward (top-down communication) - Examples of good and poor performance

A study conducted by Watson Wyatt Worldwide in the United States and Canada between 2000 and 2004 found that companies with good internal communication with their workers financially surpassed their competitors by up to 57%.

The CEO of an organization we worked for could not understand why a member of his direct team said he did not have a clear vision of the direction of the company after talking about the strategic vision for many hours on a recent *off-site*. It is clear that the manager required a different kind of clarity or degree of detail, from that which the CEO had in mind.

Following the example of *Google*, many companies have *TGIFs* ('*Thanks God It's Friday*') every Friday. These are informal meetings where all the employees and managers engage in a question-answer conversation and talk about the weekly results. To ensure that downward communication also flows well, they have implemented a series of quarterly meetings for the whole company, where the strategy is presented and the performance in the last quarter is discussed. These events are designed to celebrate the successes of the organization in the last quarter and at the same time present the objectives for the next period.

Another good example of top-down communication is *Nissan*. They make a great effort to ensure that all the regions and their employees understand what the company is going through in terms of: competitiveness, resources, strategic plans and so on. For example, after publicly announcing the results of the company, the CEO and the board of directors address their employees to explain all the details of such communication. In addition, there are meetings in all the regions to explain the situation of the company and to promote interactivity. A funny detail is that whenever there is a major milestone (sales or others), the vice presidents of *Nissan* Europe ring a bell in each of the central offices receptions to summon employees informally and tell them about it.

Nissan also uses other tools like the intranet: any department willing to tell their colleagues about what they are doing can create their own page on the intranet. In general, this Japanese brand fosters a climate of informality in a close top-down communication so that employees feel that they can interact with their managers.

Expression Chakra - The Opening English School case
Let us now explore the case *of Opening English School*, a good example to illustrate a fifth chakra that is closed or not in harmony with the others —an example of inconsistency between our expression and the rest of the organizational energy body.

In the 90s the English language training sector in Spain developed using multimedia systems and a combination of distance and presential learning techniques. The pioneer was *Wall Street Institute*, followed by *Opening English School* and others that were created or converted from traditional English teaching methods. This sector met an important need for the Spanish society, where there was little tradition in language training and where English teaching in schools was insufficient. Sheltered by this need and a more flexible and fun method than traditional language lessons, multimedia English centers flourished in Spain as a major business. *Opening English School* was created in 1996 by *Centro de Estu-*

dios CEAC (leaders in distance learning in Spain since the 50s) and a former director of *Wall Street Institute*. They rapidly grew to reach 146 centers with about 80,000 students, and a turnover of 90 million euro. *Opening*'s teaching method was based on a good academic methodology that offered positive results. They used multimedia tools that facilitated listening and speaking skills ("learn like young children, just by listening and repeating"). There were also group tutoring sessions (lessons) and voluntary grammar books that were simple but sufficient. No doubt this method could help many people overcome their difficulties when learning English through traditional methods and the discomfort of rigid timetables. The flexible hours, together with the existence of a personal academic tutor, gave clear advantages to this learning method. In addition, schools were modern and comfortable and they had quality resources. Everything was organized to provide a good service and to become a successful business.

The problem started with an excessive desire to compete with *Wall Street Institute* for market leadership. They went into a spiral where the goal was to open more and more offices and to enroll more and more students, with much higher prices than a traditional academy. The whole organization was marketing-oriented. Communication and sales were the main factors in a company supposedly dedicated to language teaching.

This is where the expression chakra lost its balance and harmony. There was no resonance between the message and the reality. Marketing messages to sell their English courses, despite being based on real evidence and benefits, were extremely exaggerated. They moved from a more "convenient" to a completely "effortless" method for learning English, from semi-presential programs to "come when you want". Information desks at the centers where replaced with aggressive sales people working to targets. The relatively inexpensive advertisements on urban billboards quickly shifted to the radio and then to the television. Advertising budgets soared, adding spaces on television and the radio, with contests, gifts and aggressive monthly promotions to close more contracts. Each teaching school had at least two well-paid salespersons with sales-based incentives. They provided information to the people that the aggressive telemarketing service had sent the center with the gimmick of a "gift" or promotion ending that week. The promise of a natural, easy, and almost effortless method, the money refund in case you did not learn English, the modern and comfortable premises full of people studying happily.

They also offered a payment method in easy installments through an external financing business. The company was galloping ahead commercially and financially. Every year they promised a two-digit growth and the financial leverage to open more offices and do more marketing was high.

Eventually, many students began to complain about not getting the promised results (claiming that in order to learn it was necessary indeed to make an effort and to have a routine and a timetable). These complaints resulted in students leaving the schools and spreading the word that something was not working. The students (and the opinions of society in general) were polarized between those who thought it was in fact a good method to learn English, and the traditional method supporters, who argued the multimedia method was not effective. All this undermined the excessive marketing efforts to sell more and more. Besides, the market began to show signs of exhaustion, and although the country was not in crisis or recession, the commercial objectives were not met. Far from being intimidated, managers redoubled marketing efforts, with more aggressive communication and radical promotions. The sales people operated under a lot of pressure to get juicy bonus deals or not to be fired. In the third year, the company was 20% to 30% below the expected targets. They already had a debt of about 10 million euro and went bankrupt. The company went hoarse and died from yelling how good it was. Soon after, *Wall Street Institute* and other companies operating with the same model also closed down. The whole sector of English teaching with multimedia methods was in crisis and collapsed, dumping many workers and thousands of students who had paid for their courses or, even worse, were still paying off their monthly loan with the financing company.

Summary – EXPRESSION chakra:

Angles	What is assessed?
External communication	The external communication of our organization.
Internal upward and horizontal communication	The internal bottom-up and horizontal communication within the company.
Internal downward communication	The top-down communication within the company.

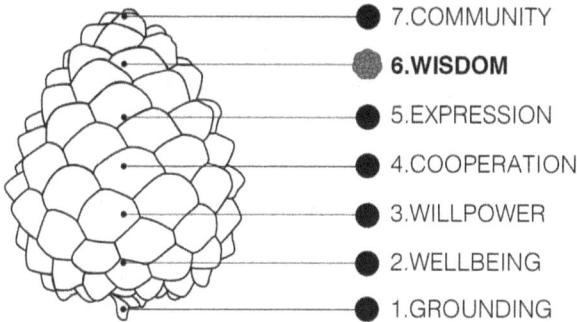

- 7.COMMUNITY
- **6.WISDOM**
- 5.EXPRESSION
- 4.COOPERATION
- 3.WILLPOWER
- 2.WELLBEING
- 1.GROUNDING

Chakra 6: WISDOM

The concept in human beings

This chakra is called *Ajna* in Sanskrit, which literally means "to perceive", "order" and "command". Its element is "light", enlightening and guiding us.

The sixth chakra, also known as the third eye, is the center of our visual, mental and intuitive perception. It is where we store our memories, we perceive our dreams and imagine our future. Through this energy center we project and see all our internal images, whether they come from memory, dreams, clairvoyance or imagination. A strong vision is the first step in transforming ethereal realities like thoughts and ideas into actual manifestations. Before we create something, we need to have a mental picture of what we are trying to create. Then we can use these images to direct our lives.

The sixth chakra is where intuition takes place. It is a skill we all have and that we use every day more or less consciously. Discerning between intuition and fantasy (understood as a non-logical perception of reality) is a recurrent process that requires our rational brain to verify and provide feedback.

The perception of reality is shaped by our mental models and our thought patterns. For instance, when we meet someone for the first time, we can quickly project images of our past, adapting them to the new situation; or we can leave our preconceived thoughts behind and observe the new reality more openly. The third eye that this chakra refers to is only opened when we are able to keep looking once our brain has recognized a known pattern in the observed. How deeply we are willing to look at something affects everything we see. At the same time, our perception has the ability to govern our reality, so this energy center refers not only to perception, but also to the decisions resulting from it.

An excessively open sixth chakra could cause a person to have hallucinations and to be unable to discern between appropriate behavioral responses and fantasies. On the other hand, when this chakra is not sufficiently developed, it may result in confusion, narrow-mindedness or insensitivity to sources of information that are not clear and do not appeal to the cognitive brain.

Parallelism in the organization

The interpretation of this chakra in the organization refers to its ability to perceive and to lead. To perceive is to obtain the necessary information to fulfill the organizational purpose and to be ahead of the times, anticipating the market trends before the society or the competition do. It also means keeping the lessons learned in our organizational memory so that they can be used in the future to make better decisions.

To lead involves, in the first place, designing a clear and compelling strategic vision and business direction; then, providing the right leadership with agile decision-making processes so that the organization moves towards that vision.

Thus, the sixth organizational chakra is composed of three angles: knowledge management (our organizational memory), strategic vision and strategic decision making.

Knowledge management:
The first angle of the sixth organizational chakra relates to knowledge management. How do we obtain, store and transmit the necessary knowledge to carry out our mission?

Let us start with the production of new knowledge. Do we research, develop or copy? Are we following the developments in our industry and in the world? Do we invest time and money to increase our knowledge of the sector and of possible future developments? Are we doing benchmarking and monitoring technological advancement? Do we attend lectures or read? If all we do is manage our day to day, assuming that the world will stay still around us, we will soon be following the squad behind the market leaders.

Documenting is another aspect of knowledge management. How do we store this knowledge? Do we have the right systems (ERPs, CRMs and others)? Do we document our key processes? Do we create *checklists*? Do we develop good business practices learned from the experience? Do we do *post-mortems* at the end of a project or key activity? Our organizational memory needs to work properly so that our strategic processes are successful. Making mistakes is only human and it should be praised in companies, because it means someone tried something new; but doing something wrong twice should not be so acceptable. If we want to avoid making the same mistake, we must be able to make this information available to one another. Many times we have seen workers in an organization reinventing the wheel every day.

The last aspect of knowledge management is the transmission and the dissemination of that knowledge. How do we use our organizational memory? Do we use processes, check-lists, best practices? If the answer is no, why? Are these processes well written? Are they designed to facilitate, rather than control, the employees' work? Do we hold internal conferences or informal chats? Are there any *mentoring* programs? How do we transfer the tacit knowledge of an experienced employee to the new staff?

In summary, the first angle of the Wisdom chakra refers to how we can manage knowledge in our organization so that it becomes a tool for improvement and progress.

Knowledge management - Examples of good and poor performance
A good example of knowledge management is the agency ACC1Ó from the Government of Catalonia (Spain), promoting business innovation, internationalization and investment in the Catalan territory. In 2006 the agency created an online platform called *l'Anella* [63] in order to fulfill that mission through knowledge management on the Internet. The project was visionary and innovative when it was created and many financial, technological and knowledge resources were invested. They wanted companies and citizens to find true value and to support their processes and decisions regarding innovation, internationalization and investment. Since 2010, we can find lots of useful information properly processed, classified and with semantic indexing: information on business and geographical communities, process management applications, meeting and exchange forums, videos and interviews, briefings of events, lessons learned, success stories and many other helpful features. This investment

of resources on online platforms could sometimes seem very high, but compared to the cost of delivering all this value to so many users through other means, it is a very productive and effective investment for the management of this type of knowledge. In fact, with a platform like this, we can achieve a level of added value that is materially and economically impossible through more traditional means. Today, more than 30,000 entrepreneurs and professionals are members of *l'Anella*, making it a large platform with a high impact among the Catalan business and economic network.

In recent decades, some popular systems for internal knowledge management have been developed that allow us to store and analyze all the information relevant to our business on the ERP (*Enterprise Resource Planning*) or CRM (*Customer Relationship Management*).

For example, consulting firms have IT platforms to document all the projects implemented with their clients. They are especially valuable and widely used by companies with several international locations. These applications safely store indexed progress reports, documents and lessons learned from each client and project. For instance, when a Sao Paulo consultant has to do a management project in the automotive supply chain market, here he can find all the information on similar projects developed in Barcelona, Chicago or Munich.

To discuss knowledge management in the context technology development, we can mention the case of *Dinamic*. This is a metal industry company dedicated to internal logistics solutions (like parcel transport in airports), where new product development is essential. A good practice in technology development implies that before we put our engineers to conceptualize and design new products, we should thoroughly research the worldwide patents to learn about the latest state-of-the-art technology. The idea is to learn from what has already been invented and work from there, avoiding legal problems for infringement of patents of third parties. Thus, since 2008 and with the support of external consulting firms and a technology center, *Dinamic* has excelled in constantly updating knowledge and accelerating R&D projects.

Strategic vision:

The second angle of the sixth chakra is vital to the success and prosperity of a project. We define the strategic vision as a paragraph describing the future of our organization. Where do we want to be in three to five years' time, for instance?

When you read the vision of the company you work for, you should be able to close your eyes and see yourself there. Therefore, a vision must be challenging and motivating while realistic and attainable. It cannot be the worst scenario for the future (very conservative) or an unattainable dream within the established deadlines (very aggressive). The strategic vision will be part of our long-term vision that will align with our organizational mission, but it must be conceived for the near future. It makes no sense to develop a long-term vision for twenty years' time unless the same vision has short-term sub-visions.

The vision document should be motivating for the employees of the organization. If we establish a very long-term vision, people may lose faith in it. If our mission was "helping conscious leaders improve the energy system of their teams and organizations" and our purpose "to facilitate organizational transformation and personal growth", our vision could be, for example: "To become an international referent in organizational change and development of the new paradigm within five years' time".

A good vision can be devised by a leader, using his intuition or clairvoyance, or it can be co-created by a team of people. Both have their own challenges. If it is an individual vision, that person will need to convince or motivate his employees and investors with it. If, for example, we want to create a vision among a group of owners or managers, the challenge will be the process we follow to agree on that vision. It should be a process of respect, genuine listening, and setting aside personal interests and egos for the common interest.

Intuition is part of the sixth chakra and it is frequently used by leaders and entrepreneurs to define the direction ahead, their vision, especially in scenarios with insufficient data or time for a more rational evaluation. Intuition is also a good tool if there is too much data, it is contradictory or can lead to multiple interpretations

In any case, the definition of a vision and the process of sharing it and encouraging our partners are right in the heart of what we mean by leadership. Leadership, individual or shared, has been widely studied and discussed. Yet there is no unanimous consensus on what it actually means to be a good leader or what good leadership is. The Center for Creative Leadership (CCL) an organization that since 1970 researches, promotes and develops leadership, defines it as the combination of three factors that have to coexist: a collective direction (vision), the alignment of people and efforts around it, and the sustained commitment of individuals to the collective success [64].

Once we have defined the vision, we must develop a set of strategic objectives on how to carry out that vision within the scheduled time. Thus, the second angle of the Wisdom chakra assesses whether our vision and strategic objectives are up-to-date, clear and inspiring.

Strategic vision - Examples of good and poor performance

In 1999 Javier Perez-Tenessa and James Hare co-founded *eDreams*, in 2012 the largest online travel agency in Southern Europe. At a conference on entrepreneurship, Javier explained that traditional travel agency experts initially believed that people would not want to buy their flights online since they did not trust the system. Again and again, they were told to abandon the project that was regarded as foolish. It was only thanks to the determination of both founders and the vision of future they created that the project prospered. By then, there were no objective facts that could help to conclude that Javier and James were right. But this is exactly the problem with historical data, in the sense that they rely on the past instead of looking into the future. Therefore, sometimes it will be essential to use past trends and analyzable market data, but most successful business projects are born of a vision based on intuition rather than analysis.

In large companies, it is not enough that the leader has a clear vision. It has to be shared and it needs to encourage all the employees.

In the 90s *Compaq* had the following vision: "We want to be one of the three major providers of computer-based tools to improve the programmer's productivity. These tools will use the increased computing capacity for improved usability."

This vision shows the company's global scope and how they wanted to achieve a leading position (one of the top three). We also see how they define their market and key value proposition (to improve the programmer's productivity), their most distinctive feature (usability), as well as the market opportunity they will rely on in order to achieve that goal. At that time, microprocessors were steadily developing and they expected an increase in their computing capacity. Thus, software applications based on powerful microprocessors could develop dramatically. That said, the vision of *Compaq* was formulated in the competitive context of the old paradigm: competition versus Cooperation. Now they would most likely rewrite it.

To conclude this section, we will see how a company in the equipment sector stated their vision: "We want to double the value of our business every five years. To generate a significant amount of our revenue in foreign markets or currencies. To offer our shareholders an attractive return on investment. To be leaders in the markets where we operate. To contribute to social development". We think this view looks more like a statement of strategic objectives and it lacks the strength to encourage or inspire a movement of people in that direction.

Decision making:

We have reached the third angle of the sixth chakra: decision making. How do we assess strategic decision making in our organization? Is it smooth, fast and proactive? Do we find it difficult to take decisions or take them too late? What role intuition plays in our choices? How are we able to integrate holistic (big picture) information into our decision making processes? Do we understand the difference between deciding with consensus vs buy in? Rogers and Blenko in a HBR article [65] state that what sets top performance companies apart from others is the quality, speed and execution of their decision making.

In their article *"Decision Making: It's not what you think"* [66], Henry Mintzberg and Frances Westley claim that, quite often, decisions defy the most obvious logics. The authors explain that there are many business situations where it is more efficient to use an visual or action-oriented approach. They sort out three types of situations where they recommend decision making based on think-first, watch-first, or act-first, correspondingly. For example, when the problem is clear, the data are reliable or the context is structured, problem solving based on think-first works best. Instead, they recommend watch-first when we have to combine many elements in a creative solution, when we need the commitment of others, or where horizontal communication is essential. Finally, they argue that act-first is the best decision-making strategy when facing new and confusing situations, or when complicated specifications can hinder our decision-making process.

Therefore, decision-making processes need to adapt to the present reality, so there will be situations in the same company that require one approach or the other.

On a more operational level, another aspect of decision making that is equally important, in our experience, is having clear roles and responsibilities for everyone. Knowing where our functions start and where they end (i.e. who is accountable for what) allows for creativity and avoids conflict and constant coordination between individuals, departments and business units. In our interview for the *Montesa* case (*Wellbeing* chakra),

Joan Cañellas commented: "*I think balancing the roles of the individuals and the departments of the company, and trying to put each person in the right place is one of the keys to successful management*".

In summary, the third angle of the Wisdom chakra assesses our strategic decision-making process and practices as a community.

Decision making - Examples of good and poor performance

In *Hewlett-Packard* the procurement decisions were (probably they still are) made according to established criteria known as *TQRDC*, that is, Technology, Quality, Responsiveness, Delivery and Cost. A team evaluates a supplier according to these criteria, weighing the importance of each factor in the total sum of the decision. It is a group decision process promoting the discussion of all relevant aspects. It is also useful to document why they decided to choose one provider or another.

The management team of a human resources consulting firm is a very different example of decision-making, this time based on act-first. They explained that at one point they met to discuss their strategy: "we want to grow" they decided "without developing any specific plan". And they soon got down to work so as to expand their portfolio of services. They received training in new skills and established subcontracting arrangements to outsource some of the paperwork. In three years, they had increased their turnover by 50% although they never developed a plan for it. They just decided to grow, they had the confidence and the drive, and they succeeded. We have set this example to counteract the previous one. It proves that, many times, decision making does not need to follow a Cartesian, clearly-defined pattern to produce good results. Each organization must find the processes that suit their needs.

In any case, we should try to avoid what happened at a Spanish winery. The executive board was composed by the founder and owner, his three sons and a couple or three professionals. When they met, they talked and discussed without having a clear decision-making process in mind. The loudest was, literally, the one with the greatest influence on the decision. Perhaps after long and intense discussions they reached an agreement, but if it was not carried out, the week after they would start discussing the same matter again from scratch, as if nothing had happened. There was no script or process to document where they had stopped and what was left to make the decision. And worst of all, despite having made a decision, there was no guarantee that a couple of months later, one of the board members would not bring up the subject again regardless of the decision they had

ORGANIZATIONAL ENERGY SYSTEM (OES)®

already taken. He could just say something like: "*I've been thinking about it and I do not agree*", so the board had to deal with that issue once more.

How decision making should change as an organization evolves? In a large British retailer, when the founder (who used to make all critical decisions) retired, the senior team was looking for the same type of leadership. The new CEO, instead, was more of a consensus decision maker and that created tensions and confusions among decision making and accountability.

The last example about decision making is explained in the HBR article cited earlier [65]. The authors explained that they interviewed different functions of a global auto manufacturer that was missing its milestones and reducing its sales in consequence. When they asked the question of who had accountability for deciding about standard features and color rangers for new models, found out that 83% of the marketing department thought it was them and 64% of the product development department said it was their responsibility.

Wisdom Chakra - The IKEA case:
We will now analyze the case of *IKEA*, a brand we all know well. We have used it as an example in other chakras and it is a good case to discuss the Wisdom chakra and its components.

The *IKEA* concept was born in Småland, a small Swedish rural town. In this region of Sweden, the land is poor and its people are thought to be hard-working. They live with little means and use their imagination to make the most of the limited resources available. This was the background of Ingvar Kamprad, who founded *IKEA* in 1943. They originally sold pens, wallets, picture frames, watches, jewelry, and nylon stockings, everything Ingvar thought people could need and that he could offer at a good price. In 1947 he introduced furniture in his product line and so the *IKEA* we know today was born.

In the 40s, Sweden was becoming an example of a country with a social vocation, where the rich and the poor were equally treated. It looks like *IKEA* drank from this source to make their vision, both human and strategic.

An example of this vision and of *IKEA's* 'know-how' is the "Big Thank You" event that took place in 1999. The worldwide sales of a whole day were distributed among all the employees. This decision (chakra 6), influenced by the corporate values (chakra 3), affects other levels like internal cooperation (chakra 4) and the emotional well-being of workers (chakra 2). There is also a connection with other angles of the other chakras, showing a systemic understanding of the company (chakra 7). It is a very good example of downward communication (chakra 5) and it strengthens the foundational energy with which Ingvar began his project (chakra 1). This is another example of the systemic nature of organizations.

The history of *IKEA* is full of obstacles that have put the company to the test on more than one occasion. But over many successful years, *IKEA* have been outstanding in their ability to deal with the difficulties they have been encountered, turning them into competitive advantages. They have been successful thanks to their adaptation to the environment and thanks to very good knowledge management: *IKEA* have always believed in learning from mistakes. For example, when Ingvar started selling large amounts of furniture, suppliers saw him as a threat and stopped selling to him. So in 1955 *IKEA* started to design its own furniture to avoid that pressure. Moreover, in the same year, one of the first employees came up with the idea of unassembled legs for tables to fit in a car and avoid damage during transport. Since then, they have been thinking in terms of flat packaging.

We can find other examples of how *IKEA* turned difficulting into opportunities: In Denmark in 1981, when a new law was passed to protect the environment that regulated maximum emissions allowed for the particleboard, an important component in *IKEA* products. Or in Germany in the late 80s, when the PVC plastic used to pack the products was reported to pollute the environment. *IKEA* managed to turn these obstacles into one of the pillars of their current success, making their products environmentally-friendly while improving their brand image.

IKEA is also a good referent in decision making and the development of key business processes, central aspects of the wisdom chakra. At *IKEA*, product design and development is a very important process that has three main objectives: affordable price, design and functionality. When developing a new product, the scheme includes an estimate of its costs with the idea of producing it at a low price. There are many players in the creation process: the designers, the product development group and the purchasing managers, who meet from the start to discuss materials, shapes and colors, and to choose the most suitable suppliers. *IKEA* is a model for its flat structure and its cost control system.

Product development never stops and all the suppliers are always open to improvements and further changes in their shapes or packing conditions. *IKEA* reduced the size of the *BANG* mug to improve its production and make a better use of the space in the microwave. They also made the color lighter to save money on pigments and be more eco-friendly.

The vision of *IKEA* is to be much more than their products, it is a way of selling, a philosophy. Product display in stores is important, but not just to show the products; it is a source of inspiration to their customers, offering smart decor solutions. Their vision is *"to create a better everyday life for many people"* [59]. They are aware that the customer is most important and they work to offer affordable prices with functional and design products, while increasing the emotional bond with customers adapting to their tastes and needs.

IKEA in 2013 was the market leader in the distribution of furniture and decorative items for the home, with an assortment of 12,000 products. It had over 120,000 employees in more than 300 stores around the world.

Summary – WISDOM chakra:

Angles	What is assessed?
Knowledge management	Knowledge management in our organization to facilitate improvement and progress.
Strategic vision	Whether our vision and strategic objectives are up-to-date, clear and inspiring.
Decision making	Our collective strategic decision-making process.

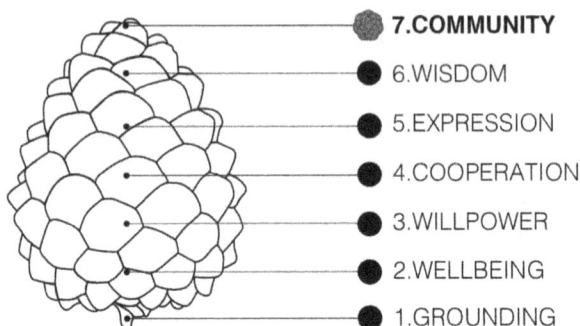

7.COMMUNITY
6.WISDOM
5.EXPRESSION
4.COOPERATION
3.WILLPOWER
2.WELLBEING
1.GROUNDING

Chakra 7: COMMUNITY

The concept in human beings

This chakra is called *Sahasrara* in Sanskrit, which literally means "1000 times, a thousandfold" and it can be translated as "abundance". Its element is "thought", the first form of consciousness manifestation.

If the first chakra was the roots in the material world, the seventh chakra is the connection of the body with the spiritual world, the heavenly, and the higher consciousness. It is through this chakra that we make our connection with others and with other systems we belong to.

The seventh chakra can also be interpreted as the operating system of our biological body. It represents the fundamental belief system on which we build our view of life and our behaviors. This deep belief system or mental "matrix" develops throughout our lives, consciously and unconsciously, especially at an early age, and it is well stored inside our brain. Thus, it is the basic structure of our consciousness. The work of the seventh chakra is to open up to the world and to higher systems. Its function is to update and reprogram this operating system with new experiences and accomplishments, and to integrate them as new patterns in the matrix inside our brain.

As we move towards the higher chakras, we transcend the limitations of the physical world to enter the world of consciousness and spirituality. This chakra gives us a global view of the system, completing (and guiding) the particular vision of the lower chakras.

A person with a closed seventh chakra will find it difficult to think for himself and will tend to follow others' leadership. On the other hand,

ORGANIZATIONAL ENERGY SYSTEM (OES)®

a person with a seventh chakra excessively open or developed will believe that he knows everything and that he is always right. Thus, he will
try to impose or dominate others with his ideas. A balanced seventh
chakra will allow for self-confidence, which also requires keeping an
open mind to expand our consciousness. Working on this chakra means
to examine and expand our consciousness by constantly enlarging our
bank of information, exploring, studying and learning.

Parallelism in the organization

We will find the parallelism of the seventh chakra in the organizational
energy system in the openness and awareness of higher systems, whether
these are the "mother" company, the industry, the community, the society
or the planet. Therefore, one of the angles of the seventh organizational
chakra is related to the organization social and environmental consciousness. This chakra includes as well the willingness to learn and to help the
organization and collaborators develop as a living organism. Finally, spirituality can be translated into the organizational world as the realization
that everything is connected and that we are all one. To this aim, we will
assess the systemic understanding in the organization.

The three angles of the seventh organizational chakra are: organizational development, social and environmental consciousness, and systemic understanding of life and its application to the company.

Organizational development
Our attitude and willingness to open dialogue, continuous learning and
organizational development will necessarily stem from the belief system
of the organization, which comes, in turn, from the basis where it was
established. It is difficult to manipulate those beliefs voluntarily, but it is
possible to develop them over time, especially with a generational relay
or other significant strategic changes.

What we need to know regarding this angle is whether the belief
system of the organization enables or limits its development as a living
organization. For instance, if the owners or managers do not believe in
the development of people, there will be no career plans or support for
employees to study and improve, personally and professionally, inside and
outside the company. Most large companies have professional development and career plans. But the question regarding this chakra should go
a little further. We must ask ourselves if the organization has a real interest

in the people and in becoming a better organization for the system. Or do we just have development plans because we need a succession plan or better economic results?

Many studies show that money is no longer a motivation for work or better results once the minimum income required has been attained. From this point, what really seem to motivate people are factors like challenge and achieving mastery in something. And this is the opportunity to grow personally and professionally. No doubt an honest development attitude will have a positive return on our employees.

As an organization, we must ask ourselves if we have an open attitude towards new and different perspectives. Pride can prevent us from learning new things. Instead, modesty helps us keep an open mind and allows the status quo to be questioned, which encourages a constant attitude of willingness for learning and innovation within organizations.

Organizations with an open attitude towards development will not only invest in formal training but will also assure on-the-job development experiences through stretch assignments, job rotations, mentoring, or building reflection time as an on-going part of the job. This, in turn, will not only assure a healthy pipeline of managers and leaders but it will also have a positive effect on employee's moral and commitment, attract the best talent to the organization, and seduce customers to their products as these values will be somehow incorporated into their Brand image.

In summary, the first angle of the Community chakra assesses our attitude and willingness to continuous learning and organizational development.

Organizational Development - Examples of good and poor performance
Larry Bossidy, a retired CEO of Allied Signal, later Honeywell and a leading executive at General Electric was quoted saying: "*I am convinced that nothing we do is more important than hiring and developing people. At the end of the day you bet on people, not on strategies.*" Today many successful leading organizations such as Unilever embrace such belief and are committed to talent development.

El Bulli, a restaurant located on Costa Brava, Catalonia, was listed for years as the best restaurant in the world. Founder and Chef Ferran Adrià explained how important it was to learn and to reinvent themselves all the time. Ferran traveled the world opening up to other realities and incorporating his findings into their offer. In 2010, when he was admired by all and he seemed to have reached the top, he decided to close the restaurant to set up a creativity center called *El Bulli Foundation* [67]. This foundation is intended to be a space where chefs can create, discuss and interact with other researchers like scientists, journalists and philosophers. A very innovative project we will no doubt hear more about.

Companies with an open mind understand that there are more talents outside the organization than inside and that they are constantly developing. This belief is the basis for the famous theory of *Open Innovation* by Henry Chesbrough [68]. Companies like *Procter & Gamble (P&G)* have implemented this practice and now more than 50% of their patents come from collaborations with people from outside the company.

Syngenta AG is a Swiss multinational in the food industry for seeds and pesticides. Created in 2000 with the merger of *Novartis* and *Zeneca*, they were unable to bring enough new products to the market to be able to achieve consistent organic growth. Then the company was reorganized towards ongoing innovation. The project was reborn with a clear commitment to the organizational and professional development that has lasted over the years. This focus on the development of the organization and its employees has helped the company to remain one of the major players in a very competitive market. Most big companies invest large sums of money in leadership development programs, succession plans, and other forms of talent management and organizational development. But, what is the philosophy behind? Quite often, it is just the need for survival. Only the most successful and lasting organizations act from the belief of human and social respect, making it an essential variable in their triple bottom line.

The real concern of pioneer organizations has led to a need to create volunteering programs as part of the development of workers and future leaders. They have realized that more and more people want to have experiences like this, and even if the return to the company is still not clear, they facilitate such programs. For example, volunteering is an important part of *Ernst&Young* corporate culture. And they are positive they are not only contributing to society by offering a pair of hands to help. This is also a way to provide their people with valuable experiences that use and enhance their professional skills.

Social and environmental consciousness:
We have used the term 'consciousness' instead of the more popular 'responsibility'. The latter, especially in Corporate Social Responsibility

(CSR), has been over-used and corrupted, in our view, by the industry and in many cases it is not authentic. It is just a cover represented by a beautiful website, a leader who speaks well in public and a pair of social actions where the focus is media attention instead of a true social and environmental contribution.

Social and environmental consciousness implies a real concern for higher systems than those of our company. In order words, it means promoting the basis for a long-lasting organization, and believing in a long-term project that must develop in harmony with the environment, the society and the planet nurturing the organization. Joan Cañellas, former CEO of *Montesa*, the case we covered in the second chakra, commented: "Ethics is always more profitable. Not only economic ethics, but also respect for high quality in production, customers, prices, partners and everyone involved."

In the first part of this book we talked about the social and environmental changes taking place in our planet. Trying to develop a business project regardless of them is an act of irresponsibility. We are positive that the free market will not allow it in the near future.

In summary, the second angle of the Community chakra assesses our attitude and the degree of responsibility towards the whole of society and the environment.

Social and environmental consciousness - Examples of good and poor performance

As we saw before, *IKEA* manufactures few of the products they sell, so they mainly depend on suppliers. To ensure the quality of their products and that all their business partners comply with their business philosophy, they have developed a code of conduct establishing the minimum requirements expected from their suppliers. It defines the social and working conditions, as well as the environmental and forestry conditions (planting and care of forests). This is especially important for the brand, as approximately 75% of the raw material for their products comes from forests.

Toms Shoes have become famous from the start with their motto: "Buy-one, Give-one" pointing to their social cause: for every purchase of a pair of shoes, they donate a pair to a developing country. The problem here is to know whether the brand is honestly doing this to help, or it is just a smart and friendly scheme to gain customers in the developed countries where they sell their shoes. Some even claim that these initiatives are not helpful at all. In a 2010 article entitled *"Bad Charity?"* [69], *Time* magazine reveals that more and more experts argue that these charitable gifts from developed countries may distort developing markets rather than help them. This could lead to an aid-dependent economic model that is unsustainable. Unfair as this appreciation may seem, it is true that the authentic social impact of a brand often occurs behind the scenes, without the bright lights of a marketing campaign.

That said, the trend is positive and we are seeing many initiatives with a genuine desire to help and contribute to the community and the environment. It would be impossible to explain them all, so we will just mention some close examples. In recent years we at Pinea3 have been actively participating in an international *Think-Tank: The Medinge Group* [70] founded in Sweden in 2000. Since 2003 they have been running an annual scheme of awards to the best social and environmental initiatives under the name "Brands with a Conscience". In 2011, the winning companies were:

Aquamarine Power [71], a UK-based company that has developed a technology to produce energy from ocean waves. They have successfully set up a large-scale demonstration facility in Scotland, proving that this sustainable alternative energy can create electricity with no emissions, and promoting a future without fossil fuels.

Caja Navarra [72] is a non-profit Spanish bank based in Pamplona that lent 3.3 billion euro and had a net profit of 200 million euro in 2008. The clients themselves decide which social causes receive the benefits and there is a policy of complete transparency. The bank staff are also encouraged to volunteer. At a time when banks are seen with skepticism and disdain, *Caja Navarra* stands out as a model of financial institution with a conscience.

Masdar City [73] in the United States is the first city with zero carbon emissions, devised to run on solar energy, without cars or skyscrapers. It has been conceived to accommodate up to 50,000 people, at least 1,000 businesses and a university. Designed by architects *Foster and Partners* and funded by the governor of Abu Dhabi Sheikh Khalifa bin Zayed Al Nahyan, it was still under construction in 2013. Phase 1 of the city should be completed by 2015, an ambitious project aimed to combine 21st century engineering with traditional desert architecture to provide safety, health and happiness.

BBC World Challenge [74], started in 2004, is a global competition to find projects or small businesses that bring real value to the market and society through innovation. *BBC* uses its power and influence to help unknown organizations that can make a difference and need projection.

TED [75] *"ideas worth spreading"* is a non–profit organization that believes we can change the world through the exchange of compelling ideas. They have created a simple but powerful mechanism: an 18-minute talk filmed and shared for free on the Internet.

Systemic Understanding:

In the second part of the book we discussed systemic understanding in detail. It is what brings us closer to the concept of spirituality in organizations. Like systemic understanding, spirituality tells us that we are all one and that every system is related to another rather than being independent units. When we understand that pouring chemicals into a river is ultimately contaminating ourselves, there will be no rational reason to do it. Systemic thinking increases our awareness about the zero-sum law within a system and helps us transition from the "I" to the "we".

A system can be defined as a set of interrelated elements that act interdependently following certain patterns and behaviors. Systemic science studies and shapes the performance of systems.

A systemic understanding will help us look and analyze issues at the root cause level, not at the symptom level. And will help us understand the action-reaction patterns within the system's laws. An anthill is a system, just like a forest, a glass-cutting machine and the global economy. And the human body is the system that inspired us to develop a model that regards organizations as living organisms: the Organizational Energy System (OES)®. This systemic approach can improve the performance and prosperity of our organization, whatever the nature of our business. The company is a system, so if we understand the (energy) laws that govern it, we will have the elements to work on its development and performance.

In a mechanical system like a car, if "low engine liquid sensor" lights up in our dashboard (symptom), we could add water or look for an underlaying bigger problem (e.g. the car has a burned head gasket and water is leaking from the radiator into the cylinders). In a body system, if we can not sleep (symptom) we could take a pill or analyze why we can not sleep (e.g. we are stressed for work, relationship, or money issues) and try to fix the cause of the problem. In organizational systems we frequently address the symptom, not the its cause. If our sales are dropping, we may react with an increased marketing budget or with additional pressure to our suppliers to reduce costs instead of evaluating other malfunctioning aspects of our system (e.g. value added, cooperation, leadership, etc.).

In summary, the third angle of the Community chakra assesses to what extent we understand and apply the systemic approach in our organization to improve its performance.

Systemic Understanding - Examples of good and poor performance

When we talked about decision making in the Wisdom chakra, we saw the case of a winery with a large area for improvement in their strategic decision-making process. If we analyzed the reasons for this behavior, we could conclude that it was not a problem with the agenda, or that the solution was not to make attendees sign the agreements of the meeting. The OES systemic vision helps us see that the main problem is not usually visible to the naked eye. In this case, the problem was threefold: due to the lack of strategic vision (chakra 6), their decisions did not follow a thread and they were taken in an outburst. In one day they could go left and in the next go right. There was also a lack of trust (chakra 4) among the members of the board that was even worse than the lack of vision. Finally, and most importantly, there was a problem with authority, self-esteem and emotionally unresolved personal egos (chakra 2). Only a systemic and global vision can help us identify the real causes of problems to treat them from the root.

Let us look at another example. A telecommunications multinational we know designed a computer system that could store and work with data from up to 3 million customers. The company was growing and the number of customers was about to reach the technically maximum capacity. Instead of investing in a new system, they decided to hire experienced consultants to program new lines of code and increase the system capacity. They were doing well and within a few years, they had more than 15 million customers and over 1 million new or modified lines of code in their software. However, the system started to underperform, it was slow and complex and the IT engineers found it increasingly difficult to understand what they were doing. In the end, after many complaints from customers and after losing a significant market share, the company decided to invest in a new system.

A systemic view of the problem, considering not only the money invested but also the potential impact on customer service and financial results, would have proved the necessity to be much more proactive in the new system investment. The same could be argued about investing in staff training or in research and development of sustainable products and services. Systemic understanding is one of the most powerful 21st century strategic tools for business management.

Community Chakra - The Triodos Bank case:

Let us look at the *Triodos bank* case, very representative of the seventh chakra in all its complexity and of the angle of *social and environmental conscience* in particular.

Triodos Bank is a European independent ethical bank. The concept of 'ethical banking' refers to a set of financial institutions whose products and services are not exclusively tied to maximum profit criteria. They invest in real economy and sectors related to the well-being of people and the care of the planet, and they are transparent in their use of money. Real economy is defined as any non-speculative economic activity outside the secondary markets. The investment is made in economic activities that can generate goods or services directly and also in projects with a positive social or environmental impact. They finance fair trade companies and projects in education, culture, environmental rescue, renewable energies, biodynamic agriculture, or attention to groups at risk of exclusion, to give a few examples. They also have a number of non-participation criteria for industries that are polluting, manufacturing arms, or that do not respect human rights.

This movement, critical with the "traditional" banking systems and policies, started against the background of public corruption scandals in the United States and other international political conflicts like the Vietnam War or the Apartheid regime in South Africa. These and other conflicts with international visibility raised awareness about the fact that the management of savings and credit was completely controlled by the banks. That is, savers and the rightful owners of that money could not decide which credits were granted with their savings. Thus, funds from an NGO working for peace could end up being spent on weapons.

This is how a movement starts, seeking an alternative economy that does not prioritize growth but that manages financial resources in order to meet the citizens' needs. Therefore, transparency is an essential tool for building the reputation of ethical banking. In such entities, they audit every single penny and there is great accessibility to the information on the projects that benefit from the credit. Likewise, managers are just paid a salary, there are no millionaire bonuses. There is sometimes an annual bonus of around 300 or 500 euro, equal for all employees in all countries, regardless of their professional category, department or seniority.

Triodos Bank was established in the Netherlands in 1980, although the project had been created in 1968 by four professionals from the legal and economic world who started the *Triodos Foundation*. The bank has been growing steadily and has expanded to Europe: Belgium, United Kingdom, Spain and Germany. Companies like *Triodos Bank* have shown that ethical banking can offer excellent business opportunities. It is also a means of improving society and the whole of the planet. In fact, it is one of the few banks growing at two digits despite the crisis in the sector. Besides, it has a "solvency rating" of 14, higher than large banks with an average of 8.

As Joan Melé, Deputy Director-General of *Triodos Bank* in Spain, comments: *"I came to ethical banking after more than 30 years working in banking, where I was in charge of a bank branch for 25 years."* In his book *"Dinero y Conciencia: ¿A quién sirve mi dinero?"* [76]. ('Money and Conscience: Who does my money serve?'), Melé argues that banks do outrageous things to maximize their profits: financial engineering, speculation, casino economy, and structured funds where it is hard to tell where the money is invested. *"Speculation is the cancer of our time"*, says Joan. It is clear that this bank has a highly developed angle of social and environmental conscience (seventh chakra). The bank needs to have the angle of the resources available (first chakra) equally open and developed to make the project long-lasting and economically sustainable.

Finally, note that *Triodos Bank* also has the other two angles of the seventh chakra well aligned: as we said before, organizational development and systemic understanding are concepts of spirituality brought to business terms. In a feature interview for *La Vanguardia* newspaper, Melé commented: *"Teach your children that it is not about making money, but about making a living. We need to replace material consumption with spiritual consumption"* [77].

Summary – COMMUNITY chakra:

Angles	What is assessed?
Organizational development	Our attitude and willingness to continuous learning and organizational development.
Social and environmental consciousness	Our attitude and degree of responsibility towards the environment and the whole of society.
Systemic Understanding	The extent to which we understand and apply systemic vision in our organization to improve its performance.

PART IV

THE PINEA3 METHODOLOGY®

- Taking Action
- First Phase: Discovery
- Second Phase: Strategy
- Third Phase: Realization
- Measuring Change
- A Diagnostic Tool– P7 Assessment®
- Self-Diagnosis for Teams and SMEs
- Examples of Organizational Diagnosis

Taking Action

Coming up with some bright or accurate ideas, or describing the new reality of the century, as futuristic as it may sound, is no longer enough. A person of action and all those who want to lead an organization or their professional life will need to make a move from ideas to action.

How I can turn all these ideas and concepts into real changes in my organization or team?

The Pinea3 Methodology for transformational change and organizational healing must be understood as the final piece of the Meta-Model we described in Part II of the book. It is indeed the deepest level of specification in the model and it represents a methodological framework to be used flexibly enough to adapt it to each specific case. Some of the methodology parameters that can be easily modified are the duration of the phases, the number of participants, the order of execution of some workshops and some of their specific contents.

The methodology operates on the Organizational Energy System (OES)®, consisting of the 7 axes or quantifiable parameters that we described in detail in Part III of the book.

It is important to see transformational change as a process. To start performing actions straight away and without prior preparation is a mistake that will entail the failure of such actions or, at best, a great effort only to get poor results. This is our experience over 20 years working for many organizations in different roles. We must undergo several states or phases to direct the organization or team towards its goals and purposes. Therefore, the proposed methodology follows three distinct phases and they have to be developed in a sequence: the first is the *Discovery* phase, the second is the *Strategy* phase and the third phase is *Realization*.

Phases:

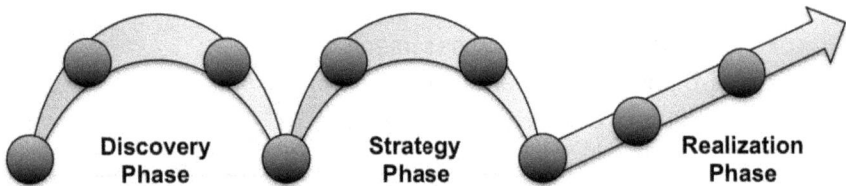

Figure 4.1

These phases are indeed three intuitive steps that are correspondingly associated to the concepts of diagnosis, the development of an action plan and taking responsibility, and finally the actual implementation. They are also the three logical stages in personal and professional development: when we realize that we have to change something (we have an "aha!" moment), we decide to do something about it and develop an action plan, and then we finally implement the change in question. We see that the third phase is potentially long, depending on the change we want to bring about.

We can observe that each phase is represented by a diagram of a crescent. We have used this model to show that each phase has a diverging and a converging part. The theory and the practice show that creative processes begin with a phase of divergence, where the most important thing is to open up our mind and make challenging associations in order to generate as many ideas as possible. Some of them might not be very realistic but they could be helpful for another person to make a powerful association that is actually implementable. This is the "craziest" stage of a creative and innovation process. The second part of the process is the convergent phase, which attempts to rationalize and make sense of the ideas that have emerged in the initial stage.

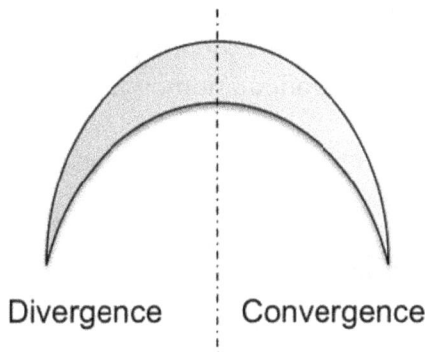

Divergence ┊ Convergence

Figure 4.2

In our approach, both phases (*Discovery* and *Strategy*) begin with a divergent group process where the phase contents give way to new possibilities. In the second part of those stages instead, we progressively define and specify those contents in the form of a diagnosis or action plan.

The dark circles in the three phases diagram (figure 4.1) represent the main workshops of the process. In the following three sections we will describe these stages and their contents in greater detail. However, it is important to note that we will describe the development of the methodology and its phases in a generic way and for a large organization of several hundred people. Obviously, the same methodology applied to small teams or enterprises can be significantly simplified. In such cases, the process should be developed with more interventions scheduled in less time. For example, we can have the first two phases (*Discovery* + *Strategy*) scheduled in a one-week *offsite*. These *offsites* (both strategic and human) can be done in the Sahara desert, in the Pyrenees or in a castle on the outskirts of Stockholm. Thus, these phases and the specific workshops should be adapted to suit each situation.

Methodological Tools

Pinea3 methodology uses an innovative combination of tools: some come from classical strategic consulting and others from the new world of organizational psychology. We focus mainly on tools addressed to manage change and people. To this aim, systemic tools are particularly powerful and useful to work with our methodology.

We specifically combine traditional business tools (360° assessments, KPIs, strategic plans and such) with experiential dynamics oriented to the development of the individual and the team (working with horses, filmed group dynamics and others). We also use group and individual *coaching* techniques (in all their methodological variations) and other systemic techniques such as configurations, which we discussed in the second part of the book.

First phase: Discovery

This is the initial phase and should always start with the person who has the highest responsibility in the organization or team, and progressively go down to the other members of the organization. It is a transformational undertaking that must be sponsored from the highest position. John McGuire and colleagues from the Center for Creative Leadership say that if you want organizational transformation you have to transform the executive team first [78]. Our more than 20 years of experience working with many leaders, executives and organizations at large in transformation projects tells us that same. The upper levels in an organization open up new spaces so that those who are at lower levels can evolve without fear, in a safe environment that is already created. In this phase the creation of a group begins. This group will be composed of like-minded people, determined to change and to lead internally. We will call this group of people Transformational Agents.

Objective:

The main objective of this phase is to achieve a consensual, broader and deeper organizational self-knowledge. This will also require the team to be aligned in improvement factors within the organization, to keep a positive development attitude and to increase the sense of belonging and the complicity between its members.

The objectives of this phase are achieved through the development of a diagnosis of the organization or the team, based on the 7 axes of the Organizational Energy System (OES)®. As we saw in Part III of the book, each of the axes is divided into three complementary angles. Therefore, 21 issues are discussed and assessed to reach a consensus. The assessment identifies the opportunities for improvement unfolded by each of the 21 angles, distributed in 7 axes (chakras). Thus, the resulting diagnosis provides a comprehensive and holistic vision that is jointly approved by the participants.

Interventions:

The development of this phase with a senior management group of a medium or large organization can last two or three months (even longer if there are agenda constraints or pressing priorities). We always recommend compressing it to six weeks, if possible. For smaller teams the phase can be realized in less time, even in a single two-day workshop, for a group of approximately ten people.

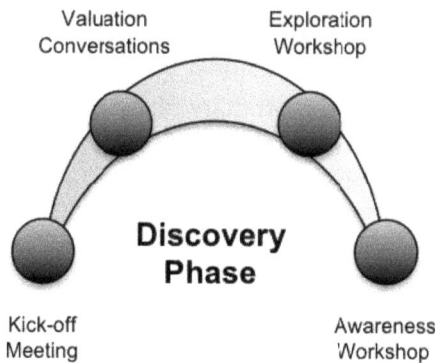

Valuation
Conversations

Exploration
Workshop

**Discovery
Phase**

Kick-off
Meeting

Awareness
Workshop

Figure 4.3

We will now describe the four major milestones that the first phase usually runs through.

Kick-off Workshop. After some initial planning meetings, the phase begins with a formal kick-off, which explains the methodology and the objectives of each phase and workshop in general. This workshop begins by building team cohesion and therefore it is important that all members attend this initial step, usually composed by the management team, the board of directors and/or the owners.

Valuation Conversations. The second step is to have a series of conversations on the Organizational Energy System (OES)® with all the participants, in groups of two or three people. This is done to start exploring team dynamics with systemic *coaching* techniques, as well as to introduce the concept of OES to managers.

Exploration Workshop. Systemic Configurations techniques are used in this workshop to treat relevant issues in the management or ownership of the organization. The head of the company, along with the systemic facilitator, will be responsible for developing the key questions to be explored in this workshop.

Awareness Workshop. This workshop represents the end of the first phase and the beginning of the second. It brings together the entire management team to discuss, evaluate and agree the 7 axes of the OES (with its 21 angles). In this workshop the techniques used are oriented to create a safe, trustworthy environment so that the participating senior executives or managers, can have access to personal spaces and open up to the rest of the team. The OES framework facilitates a safe and deep dialogue that allows the senior leadership team to "*slow down to power up*". McGuire et al. say: "*Slowing down at key times for learning, diagnosis and dialogue allows you to 'power up' – creating accurate, focused, valuable decisions*".

Since this is also where the Strategy phase begins, the workshop ends with a *brainstorming* session to start developing a list of improvement ideas that can enhance the organizational system.

Deliverable:

The actual material result at the end of the *Discovery* phase is a graph (spider web type) showing the consensual evaluation on each of the 7 axes in the OES by the whole team.

Thus, a single image (see example in figure 4.4) provides a global and systemic understanding of the organization:

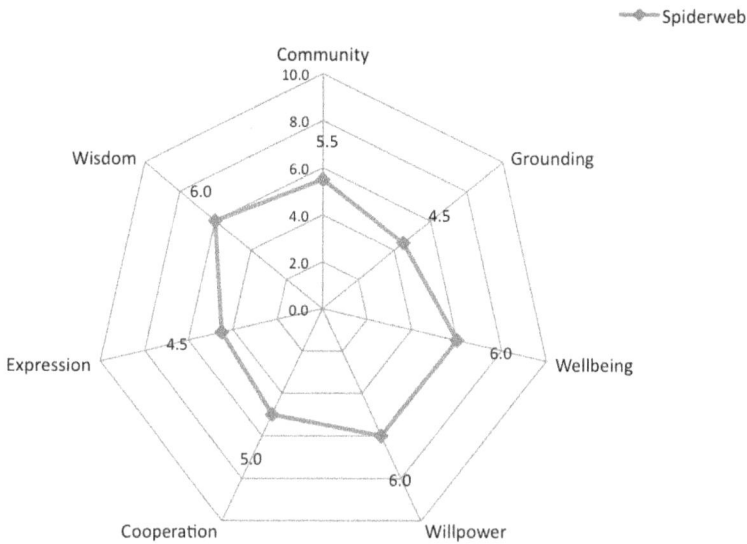

Figure 4.4

The resulting diagram and the process to get there evoke the strengths and weakness of the organization at a global/holistic level. Executive team will be able to see things that they have not seen before about their organization because the lens to look at the problems is different.

It is still early (we don't have enough data yet) to be able to statistically typify different spiderweb shapes and be able to draw conclusions in this way. But we could assert things like if an organization has an expanded first chakra and a closed seventh chakra, the organization is probably too heavily focused on the short term (e.g. quarterly financial results) and needs to improve their longer term awareness and attention. While the contrary (an organization with a closed first chakra and an open seventh) would indicate that it needs a stronger grounding, focusing on things like the value we provide to the market, sales and our financial health, and balancing that with us trying to make the world a better place.

The resulting graph can be also discussed and analyzed using the 21 variables (3 for each chakra), giving greater detail to the diagnosis and therefore to the organizational improvement plan generated from here (see example in figure 4.5). Each of the three angles within a chakra are categorized as either *neutral*, *yin* or *yang* components. We will expand these concepts and level of analysis in future publications as we are still collecting relevant data. If you are interested in this, please contact us.

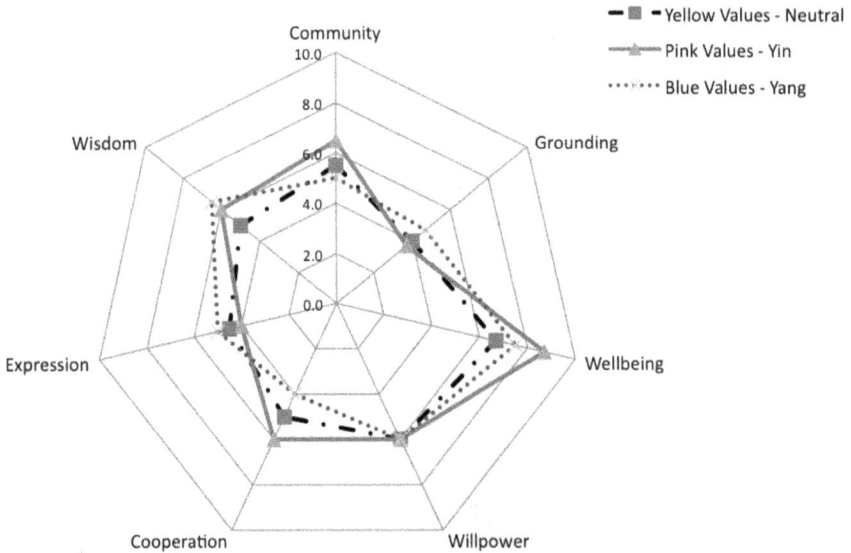

Figure 4.5

While this is the most objective and visible deliverable, there are other very important results of the discovery phase. At the end of this first phase, the beginning of a transformation in the team is already noticeable. The space created for dialogue and learning as equal humans is noticeable in their relationships, their communication, and their willingness to cooperate and to build a common project from the heart.

Second phase: Strategy

The second phase of the methodology is essential to the effectiveness of the transformational change process. It links the organizational awareness (*Discovery*) with the executive change implementation (*Realization*). In this phase actions are designed and integrated into the business strategy of the organization. Participants assume responsibility, commitment and leadership in the implementation of the desired organizational change.

This phase requires having a mission, vision and a strong set of values that are defined and shared across the organization. When they are outdated, not shared or inexistent, the workshops of this phase will also address their development.

We used to call this phase *empowerment* as it is related to empowering the senior leadership team to plan an implement the desired change instead of leaving the process as a pure mental exercise and fall short of seeing its benefits. This phase could be also called *organizational leadership* as it encourages and helps the executive team to live the change from the top down. In this phase the *leadership strategy* is defined and agreed upon as a key success factor going forward.

Objective:

To achieve personal commitment and organizational alignment from the executive team in the implementation of leadership strategies and action plans designed to enhance the performance and prosperity of the organization. This entails developing a strategic plan or improving the existing one, as well as developing a specific leadership plan/strategy with measures and follow-up indicators that capture the essence of what you want to change in the organization. This plan, which we call *Organizational Prosperity Plan (OPP),* must contain business actions (*hard*) and people-oriented actions (*soft*). In other words, we must complement *what* to do with *how* to do it?

The executive team also agrees on a set of leadership behaviours that they will exemplify as role models. In addition, the development of the OPP allows integrating the concepts of Prosperity (profit, people and planet) in the day-to-day business reality.

Interventions:

During this phase, the initial group (for instance, 15 people) is enlarged to double the number. Each participant is asked to choose a person from their team to be incorporated to the process, thus descending a level in the organizational hierarchy.

The typical duration of this phase with a team of 30-40 people is a quarter.

Figure 4.6

This phase usually goes through the following milestones:

The *Awareness workshop* was explained in the *Discovery* phase as it is somewhere in between the two phases. Thus, the *Strategy* phase formally begins during the *Awareness workshop*.

Extension Workshop. This workshop is made with a new group of people that are incorporated here into the process, in order to increase the number of participants and go down one level in the hierarchy. The members of this new group usually belong to the direct teams of the management board that participated in the *Discovery* phase. During this workshop they are introduced to the Pinea3 methodology, the OES and the global self-diagnosis of the organization.

From this moment, the team of Transformational Agents is composed of the initial group plus this extended group, forming a single team of internal Transformational Agents. All the future workshops in this phase are developed jointly for the join group.

Integration Workshop. This workshop starts the development of the Organizational Prosperity Plan (OPP). It revises and enhances the organization's strategic plan in the light of the lessons learned in the *Discovery* phase. A real example of the modification of a strategic plan (the 'what') is adding to the original objective: "to develop new products with higher added value", this additional information: "especially those that contribute the most to the protection of the environment". A real example of the change (in 'how') is "to rationalize labor costs" (in the original plan) "with full recognition and respect for people, seeking their best possible situation" (modified).

If the organization does not have a defined strategic plan or system and has to start developing it from scratch, a series of additional workshops could be conducted. It is also possible and quite common in these workshops to review the purpose, mission, vision and values of the organization or team. In both cases, the work is done in the light of what was learned in the previous phase so that the notion of purpose has more strength and the conceptual contents are more aligned with what we have called the new paradigm.

Commitment Workshop. This workshop presents and reviews the OPP and ensures the public commitment of the participants in the strategic implementation plan. Participants also agree to make personal improvement changes that they have chosen themselves.

During this phase the group identifies potential barriers to the implementation of the OPP and identifies the group's needs to help them overcome these barriers, giving rise to the next phase, *Realization*, which is launched in this workshop.

Accompaniment. In this stage it is possible that some people face important challenges, like new personal and professional changes. They also could face personal challenges that each of them has chosen for himself/herself to work on. Experience tells us that it is very important to provide executive accompaniment (*coaching*) to help some individuals to achieve their goals.

Deliverable:

The actual result of the *Strategy* phase is a strategic plan document (OPP) inspired by the OES. The layout and level of sophistication will depend on the initial degree of definition the organization or team starts to work with.

We do not attach any examples of Organizational Prosperity Plan (OPP) as each organization is unique: Some use the *Key Performance Indicators* (KPI) by Robert Kaplan, others use highly detailed and customized Excel sheets or just PowerPoint presentations.

Third phase: Realization

This phase of the Methodology responds to the plan developed during the *Strategy* phase and focuses on the needs identified in the *Discovery* phase. Therefore, this stage is really tailor-made to suit each situation so that the desired change or improvement spreads throughout the organization and becomes visible also from outside (customers, suppliers, market and all stakeholders). In large organizations, this is achieved by significantly increasing the number of Transformational Agents and working progressively towards the lower levels. In this phase we typically include a leadership development program that complements other team and organizational interventions (e.g. customer orientation or feedback), which are more focused on developing practical management skills.

Objective:

The objective of this phase is twofold: On the one hand, it seeks to ensure that the change sticks into new organizational behaviors. For that to happen, the energy of the company's transformational change process must continue to flow and evolve, increasing the number of people and business levels involved. Complementary, this phase also aims to improve the staff's leadership and management skills (e.g. emotional intelligence, listening and decision making), as well as their attitudes and behaviors (e.g. proactivity, responsibility and creativity), so that the organization can move towards higher levels of prosperity. Obviously, the skills and attitudes to develop will depend on the specific needs identified in the *Discovery* phase.

In some instances (typically some large companies) this phase is managed internally and the company itself provides a group of qualified people to develop the programs, workshops and activities systematically. In this case our work is training the trainers and the executive support discussed below or any other complementary aspect to the customer capabilities and desires.

Structure:

As this phase is tailor-made to suit each organization, it is important to describe the methodological framework used to design it. The *Realization* phase, unlike the two previous phases, is not represented by a crescent but by a ramp up line (see figure 4.1). This is because it does not have a diverging and a converging part like the previous ones, and also because it represents the continued growth of the organization.

The development and growth processes are indeed not continuous or linear, but they ascend similarly to a spiral. Many authors have described the process of spiral growth on a personal level (e.g. *The 12 Stages of Heal-*

ing [79], *Changing for Good* [80], *Spiral Dynamics* [81]), also applicable to organizational and team development. The three phases presented here: Discovery, Strategy and Realization, should be understood as part of a larger spiral growth. Thus, they constitute a cycle, a growth process much more chaotic by nature, where the 'realization' begins with the 'discovery' or where 'moments of awareness' (discoveries) occur along the process and not only during the first stage.

Conscious that development processes are not linear, we decided to use an ascending line to represent the third phase. This simplifies the model and facilitates the understanding of the concept of *intensity* in the *Realization* phase. The *intensity* is represented by the slope of the ramp. It is clear that if we want to reach a certain level of performance, prosperity, organizational health, or whatever you may call it, we need to work on a conceptual level to bring the ascending line to the desired state. Therefore, this ramp has a certain slope (gradient or angle) and a specific duration. If we want to get really high, we will need to go up faster and/or lengthen the rise for longer. These are the two main parameters we can play with at this stage: intensity and duration.

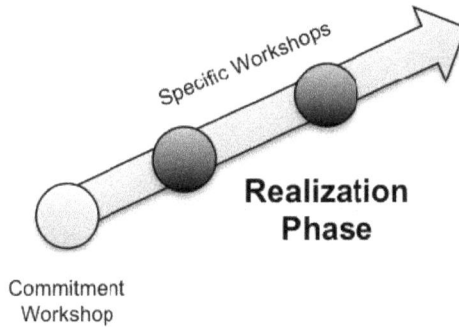

Figure 4.7

The intensity of the *Realization* increases if we increase the number of interventions. This phase typically rolls out one (or more) leadership development program(s) for management functions but it also emphasizes individual contributor skills training. This this in mind, in this phase we talk about '*beats*' instead of workshops, which is the basic intervention unit in this part of the methodology. A *beat* consists of a 4-hour training, typically for a group of 15 up to 25 people. *Beats* can have a variety of contents, as shown below, but typically focus on practical skill development and their application to the work context.

The number of *beats* per quarter and the number of people participating in each *beat* indicate the intensity of this phase. If you want a more intense and rapid change, you can increase the 'strength' of the phase. Thus, each organization or team can choose the speed to achieve the transformational change pursued, always within reasonable maximum and minimum margins.

The methodology to design a high impact work plan relies on a two-fold classification of *beats*. These are structured according to the energy level on which they work and also according to the group they are addressed to (senior executives, management level, middle managers, technicians, individual contributors, etc.). In this way you can design specific actions suited to the content and the recipients. All the *beats* must be designed following a global strategy and an intervention logic that makes them complementary and synergetic.

The *beats* are then classified according to the type of energy they unlock and therefore they mainly follow the OES structure: Grounding, Wellbeing, Willpower, Cooperation, Expression, Wisdom and Community. We must remember the systemic nature of the organization to emphasize that the *beats* do not work on isolated compartments, but they usually have an effect on more than one at the same time. When planning the intervention, we should take into account the effect of the combination of *beats* at different levels, for a greater efficiency with the resources available.

The *beats* are based on training content, common in leadership development and personal growth, and they are adapted to the reality of the organization. Some examples of the *beats* used are: assertive communication, listening and feedback, managing by objectives, collaborating in diversity, the leader-coach, delegating and empowerment, managing emotions and conflict, win–win decision making, and conscious leadership. The contents of each *beat* are designed to move certain energies and increase the capacity of the organization as a system.

Alongside the completion of *beats* in the organization, it is important to keep the motivation and commitment of the original team of internal transformational agents (participants from phases 1 and 2). They are the leaders and sponsors of the process so re-energizing *beats* with the initial executive team are used to ensure that the process of change continues to be led from above and to be led by example. These re-energizing *beats* are frequently combined with the custom-made leadership development program that is rolled out during this phase.

The minimum duration of this phase is two quarters, although the recommended duration is four quarters or more, depending on the type and size of organization and the degree of change you want to bring about. It is advisable to assess the progress regularly through specific indicators that show the evolution of the organization.

Intervention:

At the beginning of the stage, the work plan is decided for the next two quarters based on:

- Needs to be covered. We rely on the diagnosis of the *Discovery* phase and the needs expressed during the *Strategy* phase.
- The business areas and organizational chart levels where we want to act.
- The 'intensity' of the phase, which is also a function of the priority we give to change and of the budget available.

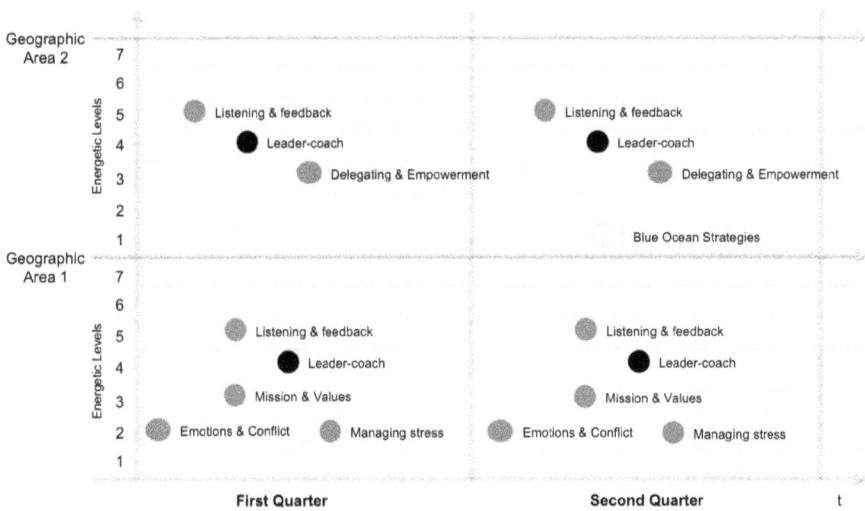

Figure 4.8

This example of work plan corresponds to a company with several production plants in different areas. There are four things to note here:

- The two geographic areas are treated with a different intensity and content based on their specific development requirements.

- The different shades (colors) of the *beats* indicate the type of audience they are intended for (high potentials, middle managers, executives, etc.).
- The location of the *beat* on the horizontal axis corresponding to the scheduled timing of the workshops.
- The repetition of workshops in the first and second quarter is meant to reach all the people these interventions are addressed to. This process can be repeated several times, changing the intensity and the content of the *beats* if necessary.

Executive accompaniment

During this phase, it is highly advisable to provide executive coaching processes (*coaching*) to some key players, as this greatly enhances the process of organizational change. In fact, in some cases it is essential to offer this type of work to unblock certain situations, individuals and energies. Providing a quality executive *coaching* is especially important for people with great challenges.

Furthermore, we have experienced a very positive effect when management offers coaching services to key employees in the organizational change process. This additional support constitutes an aid to individuals, whether the issues discussed with the coach are purely organizational or include personal matters. The result is always a very powerful and transformative effect in people, who can feel the full support of the organization as individuals and not just as managers of a function or area. The return to the organization is usually much bigger than if the coaching is just oriented to specific objectives, since the manager incorporates these goals by his own choice (with responsibility and gratitude) and not as an imposition.

The incorporating of an executive mentoring program for individuals is certainly a key aspect for successful transformational change processes.

Deliverable:

The actual result of the *Realization* phase is change itself. But how can we objectively measure that change? In the business world it is important to quantify the changes; so we will explain how to do it in the next section.

In summary:

Figure 4.9

Measuring change

There are several ways to measure the success of organizational transformation. Some are more scientific and others more common sense and best practices in business. Let us look at three possible ways to measure the impact of a change process: the scientific way, through business indicators, and with more simple techniques such as observation and common sense.

Scientific

The most scientific (and objective) way to measure a process of organizational change is through an evaluation questionnaire to be passed before and after the interventions, and even once a year if the process takes several years. To obtain a reliable scientific measurement, the number of people answering the questionnaire should be a representative sample of the organizational body we want to work on. We also need a sufficient number of participants to use quantitative statistical analysis methods.

This means having a representative sample of the organization with at least 100 people participating in the process and answering the questionnaire before and after the change interventions. The questionnaire could be developed specifically or be an existing and already validated questionnaire. The questions measure those changes we are intending to assess in the organization, whether that is employee engagement, product innovation or employee turnover. Although it is not an irrefutable proof, this is the most scientific and accurate method that can be used to assess whether these interventions are changing the organization and its teams in a visible way.

In the next section we present a diagnostic tool ($P7Assessment^{®}$) we have developed at Pinea3 that scientifically measures the impact of this methodological change. It is an assessment tool that can be used with both internal and external collaborators or even with customers.

Indicators

Another way to measure the impact of a change process like the one proposed here is to develop a number of business indicators. There can be more or less indicators and they can be more or less quantifiable.

For example, a company might include in its list of indicators: cooperation between departments, customer satisfaction and EBITDA. The latter is easy to measure, while measuring the first two requires developing a way of gathering information from our staff and customers.

These indicators can be developed before starting the first stage of the change process (*Discovery*), but in most cases they are developed at the end of this stage, or even at the end of the second phase (*Strategy*). The reason for this is that owners and executives do not have a complete (systemic) understanding of the problem from the start and they can only see the symptoms. We know that we are losing market share or that sales are going down, but we cannot tell if this is because our sales team is not well trained, because our products and services are not suited to the market, or because our staff is not motivated; or maybe because of a combination of these and other things.

In this case, if management chooses the business indicators before starting the process, it is easy for them to just think of measuring market share or sales volume. The challenge of doing so is that these measures are the end result (symptoms) of the real problems. As the Pinea3 methodology is always intended to address the underlying problems, there is a time lag until the symptoms are relieved.

Thus, one of the challenges of this measurement method is that the indicators chosen should be able to capture changes in the organization that are visible in the short or medium term at the most. And we should also measure these indicators before the process so as to compare them with the results a posteriori. Looking at the development of these indicators in more detail, we can see they are not far from the scientific method we mentioned before. Therefore, we can also use the *P7Assessment®* as a standard tool of business indicators and to measure the global organizational health. Furthermore, as we will discuss in the next section, this tool can incorporate a number of custom indicators or questions.

Observation

This is the easiest and most straightforward method, and probably the most commonly used in organizational development. It frequently uses measuring methods banned for Science, like personal observation, individual feelings and intuition. However, if the work has been truly transformative, you can sense it and feel it in the atmosphere.

A very widespread measurement method is conducting questionnaires after each of the workshops or intervention, also known as *happy-sheets*. The term is self-explanatory, as they assess how happy participants are after the workshop. These questionnaires measure participant satisfaction "in the heat of the moment", but they are not a useful measure for assessing real change in the organization or the people answering it. One thing is how satisfied they are with the "course" and another thing is what behaviors they are able to change from that moment onwards. In fact, it is very common to find workshops where people feel thrilled after a really inspirational session, but most of them will be unable to take any of the ideas into practice. Instead, there are other interventions where participants end up internally frustrated and shaken because the workshop has affected their ego, but have a much more transformational effect although participants failed to see its positive effects in its immediate evaluation.

What is more, some scientific studies point out that if the participant does not face a real challenge, the "training" is not transformative and fails to affect any behavior on the participant. Quite often, the attendees will write down lots of things on their notebooks only to store them on the shelf and forget about everything, so we should be careful not to give too much attention to the assessments given right at the end of the workshops. It is better to wait for a few days or weeks and then send the questionnaire to the participants to assess its effect after the initial emotions are gone.

Diagnostic Tool - P7Assessment ®

The *P7Assessment*® is an organizational assessment tool that measures the inner health of an organization from the seven OES variables. It is developed as an on-line questionnaire with 42 multiple-choice questions and is available in many languages.

This tool has several possible uses as detailed below:

- As we noted in the previous section, this tool can be used to measure the impact of the change process following the Pinea3 methodology. It is less appropriate to use for a different change methodology, as it is adapted to the parameters of the Organizational Energy System (OES)® this methodology works with.
- Moreover, the *P7Assessment*® is also useful for owners and general managers or human resource managers, individuals and organizations that want to know more about the internal state of their organization from a systemic point of view. From there, it will be possible to design a series of interventions to improve the state of the organization, if necessary. Many companies realize where they are, but they recognize that, for one reason or another, they are not prepared to face a process of change and organizational development at the time. Even in these cases it can be interesting to have a "snapshot" of the company's internal health.
- This diagnostic tool is also especially useful for improving our company's strategic plan (in its annual review, for example). Its use for this purpose will provide a more complete view of the organizational system and allow us to generate improvement actions, ideas and projects from a more global perspective.
- We can measure as well the climate of our organization and the strength of our corporate culture. With this tool we can evaluate the business environment from a holistic perspective, since it does not focus on problems in a specific department, but on the global vision of the organization each one has from their department.
- In addition, it is useful to learn about the image of our brand in the market from the point of view of customers and other stakeholders, when used with this group of people.
- Finally, it is also a helpful tool to request and receive valuable *feedback* from the first line management anonymously and not focusing on the individual but on the business.

The *P7Assessment*® information is received through a custom report that reflects the responses graphically. It is possible to segment and group the answers according to region, business unit, department, management level or other factors, as long as there are enough participants.

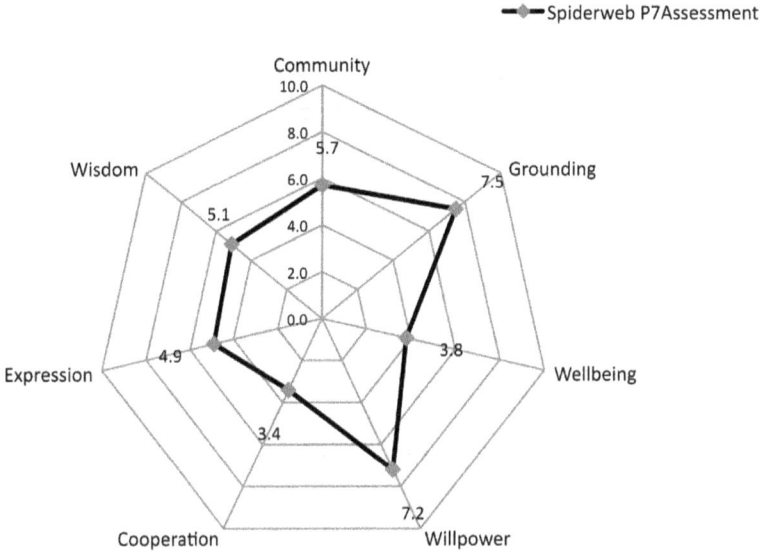

Figure 4.10

The 42 questions are actually statements that must be assessed on a scale from 1 to 7 depending on whether we agree with the statement to a greater or lesser extent (strongly agree, somewhat agree…). As an example, here are some of the questions of the tool that are formulated as statements:

- I have freedom of action in my job and I can manage myself within my responsibilities, there is no excessive control.
- The organization and workers react positively to new situations and adapt to change easily.
- The mission and purpose of the organization bring light to me and give me strength to do my daily work.
- In my organization there is an atmosphere of trust.

The *P7Assessment*® is a flexible tool that allows adding other custom questions to make the most of the survey. In this way organizations can design key questions that are specific to their business model and organizational reality.

Self-Diagnosis for teams and SMEs

Due to the small number of people in a team or a small and medium enterprise, it is not suitable to develop the phases described above with too much depth and rigor.

How can a team or SME diagnose their Energy System? Here we provide three steps to follow and a questionnaire-guide that can be used for this purpose.

How small or how big does my company have to be in order to use these steps? Teams formed by three people or more can use this methodology adapted to teams, adjusting it to their reality in every case. Regarding the maximum number, it is not as clear and it somehow depends on the type of activity and of personnel we have. A medium-size company of 200 people, with a productive activity located in a factory and with a large number of operators is not the same as a company providing services, with the same number of employees, but in this case more qualified and distributed in several countries. The first company probably has a team of managers and middle managers of less than 25 people and it is suitable to treat it as a team. In the second case, due to the potential complexity of the business, geographies and the relative importance of each employee, it might be better to develop the complete methodology with the three phases described above.

Thus, the methodology unfolded in these lines is intended for a group of 5 up to 25 people, which is what we consider a standard number to be treated as a team.

First step:

First, we need to clearly define the team or "energy body" we want to work on. It can be a natural team (e.g. the sales team), a cross-functional team (e.g. the ERP implementation team), a division (e.g. the wiring business unit) or an entire organization. Thus, it is possible to include, where necessary, franchisees, shops, distributors, the founder, the board of directors or certain strategic partners. It is important to define the team

THE PINEA3 METHODOLOGY®

at the beginning of the process so that all the assessments refer to the same "living organism".

Second step:

The second step is to evaluate each of the 7 axes, energy centers or chakras of the team. These assessments can be made with the *P7Assessment®* tool individually and anonymously or directly through a meeting with the whole team. The mechanics of the meeting is to agree on a group assessment for each of the 7 axes of the questionnaire attached at the end of this section.

As we have seen above, the 7 assessments can be represented in a spider web diagram. Each axis or chakra contains 3 elements and therefore the overall assessment may be more or less influenced by those aspects we consider the most important for us at that time. Just use your common sense to agree on an global rating for each axis.

The ratings always have a value from 0 to 10. There are countries like Spain, where the marks in school and college are also expressed from 0 to 10; 5 for pass, 6 for good, and so on. When we do these ratings, it is important not to think in terms of fail–pass, but in the space for improvement that is left available. So, if we value a certain angle or axis with a 4, we are not failing it, but we are acknowledging that there is more room for improvement and that there is still a long way to go. On the other hand, if we choose a score of 8 or 9, it means that there is very little room for improvement. A rating of 10 represents the best mark possible for our team in this particular issue at this particular time. We are not comparing ourselves with any other team that could be a role model.

It is important for participants to focus on areas or opportunities for improvement in the organization, rather than to establish a static rating or assessment of our past. This will promote a positive attitude, guide us into the future and enable us to take improvement actions.

In this process the discussions and arguments that have led us to raise or lower our evaluations are more important than the ratings themselves. These considerations will be very important to continue with the third step of this process.

It should be pointed out that the team leader, the owner, the general manager or other members in top positions should be able to leave their stripes outside the room for the process to be truly effective. They should behave as one more member of the team which is indeed difficult at times.

Third step:

In view of the figure resulting from the previous stage (*spider web* diagram), the third step is to develop some ideas to improve each of the 7 axes. We will use all the notes and considerations mentioned and we will focus mainly on the lower ratings in our system.

This exercise should be a *brainstorming* session, with all the rules and best practices for this type of activity. We recommend three simple and basic rules: 1) eliminate hierarchies, 2) prohibit the NOs, the BUTs and any other comments that repress creativity like "this will not work", and 3) the quantity is more important than the quality; at this stage, the aim is to fill sheets with ideas. These ideas will be more or less applicable but what could be a "crazy" idea up front, can be used to make a connection for somebody else generating an idea that is less crazy. From that point, a third person may be able to take that raw idea and ground it in something truly out of the box but with great applicability. This is how team creativity actually works!

Improving from self-diagnosis

The next step will be to condense all these ideas of the third step in a smaller list that is more focused and that can be carried out. This part of the process consists of grouping ideas by topic to assess them so that the winning ideas can become specific projects or actions. It is a prioritization process that will take us to rationalize the list of ideas that we want and that we can carry out at this time. These actions can be either focused on the strategy or on the people.

We should also document, for each action we want to perform: a more or less detailed description of the project, a leader, an estimated investment or budget required, a priority and an estimated timing.

We need to highlight the importance of assessing the progress of our projects as well as the changes and improvements in our team resulting from them. An easy way to evaluate progress is to carry out the assessment questionnaire described in the second step after a while. It is detailed below.

Questionnaire for teams:

These are the questions or assessment areas that the team can be asked for self –diagnosis using the systemic Pinea3 methodology.

Axes or chakras	What is assessed?
Chakra 1 - Grounding: *Foundational energy* *Value Added* *Resources available*	Do we take the time required to establish ourselves as a team? Do we provide real value to our organization/market? Do we have the people and the budget needed to carry out our mission?
Chakra 2 - Wellbeing: *Emotions* *Adaptability to change* *Brand image*	Is there a good atmosphere between us? Do we embrace change easily? Do we have a good image outside the team/company?
Chakra 3 - Willpower: *Purpose and Mission* *Values* *Power*	Do our purpose and mission give us strength and guidance? Are we consistent with our values (written or not)? Have we found the balance between control and delegation?
Chakra 4 - Cooperation: *Cooperation with external entities* *Internal cooperation* *Customer relations*	Do we truly cooperate with our environment (external partners, suppliers, competitors)? Is there trust between us? Do we provide a good service to our customers (internal or external)?
Chakra 5 - Expression: *External Communication* *Internal upward and horizontal communication* *Internal downward communication*	How do we communicate externally? How do we communicate internally? Do we listen to each other?
Chakra 6 - Wisdom: *Knowledge Management* *Strategic Vision* *Decision Making*	Do we manage our knowledge properly? Do we have a clear and inspiring vision of where we are headed? Are we efficient in group decision making?
Chakra 7 - Community: *Organizational Development* *Social and environmental conscience* *Systemic understanding*	Do we have an attitude and willingness to continuous learning? What responsibility do we take in our social and environmental impact? To what extent do we understand and apply systemic understanding to improve the performance of our team?

Any team manager, division manager or SME owner can carry out the self-diagnosis we propose here.

Examples of organizational diagnosis (Discovery phase)

Here we present three company examples inspired by real cases.

Global industrial company - automotive sector

Company A is a manufacturing company that produces electronic and mechanical assemblies. It has 5,000 employees and production plants in 10 countries.

At the time of the *Discovery* phase the company was facing several significant challenges. The survival of the company was threatened by financial issues. They were then considering an important and strategic merger/acquisition. The management team we worked with was in charge of a division made up of three countries and a number of production plants. All their first level managers had just joined the division and needed a period of acceptance and adaptation. The speed of business and the critical financial situation did not allow for delays or mistakes.

Thus, the challenges faced were mainly: the consolidation of the new management team at a large division in a business environment of high uncertainty and high levels of pressure at a personal level.

The graph below shows the diagnosis resulting from the analysis based on the 7 axes of its energy system (OES). As can be seen, certain energies flowed well, while others had serious restrictions (mainly the Willpower and Expression axes).

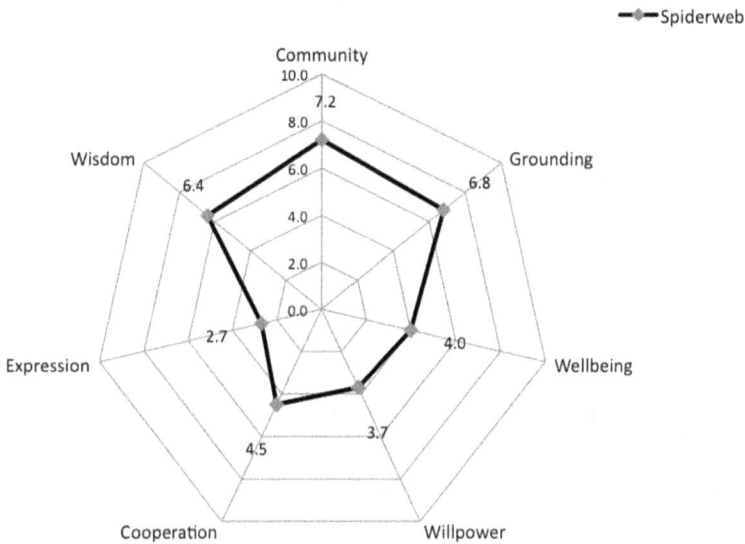

Figure 4.11

The reality behind this representation is that of an organization with poor internal communication capacities and poor communication to the market (Expression axis). The company devoted many efforts to new product development and to productive efficiency, but invested very little in improving internal communication. Although communication was not an ultimate goal for any of the participants or the company, they agreed that poor internal and external communication was a major obstacle to the development of their functions in a very complex environment.

The spider web diagram also indicated that some basic elements of corporate culture and its values had been temporarily "forgotten" for a few years, due to the serious crisis and the critical moments the company had undergone. This was negatively affecting the Willpower and Wellbeing axes. The team expressed their consensus that this point was the one that most affected their motivation and commitment to the business project.

In this case, the diagnosis gave much inner strength to the management team, despite its recent creation, as it allowed them to agree on who they were as a team, what challenges they faced together, and the areas of priority. As they commented, without a complete and holistic guide of the organization, it would have taken them many months of endless arguments to reach the same point of consensus and action orientation and still they would not have reached this status.

From the very next day after the development of this diagnosis, the managers began to behave differently in an observable way. They also reminded each other about their commitment to the values that they wanted to keep despite the harshness of the environment.

National service company

Company B is a service company related to the insurance sector. It has 1,000 employees and provides coverage nationwide through regional offices and delegations.

At the time of the *Discovery* phase the company was facing strategic challenges arising from structural changes in the industry that forced an operational and business reorientation. All this was lead by a new CEO who had been assigned this complicated task.

At the initial stage of the process with Pinea3 methodology, the CEO had devised a plan to completely restructure operations and he wanted to ensure that the change took place in the people as well as the processes. He had a clear plan and he needed the management to join him in his strategic proposal. The CEO knew that his managers needed to explore the situation and share a reliable basic diagnosis so as to improve together.

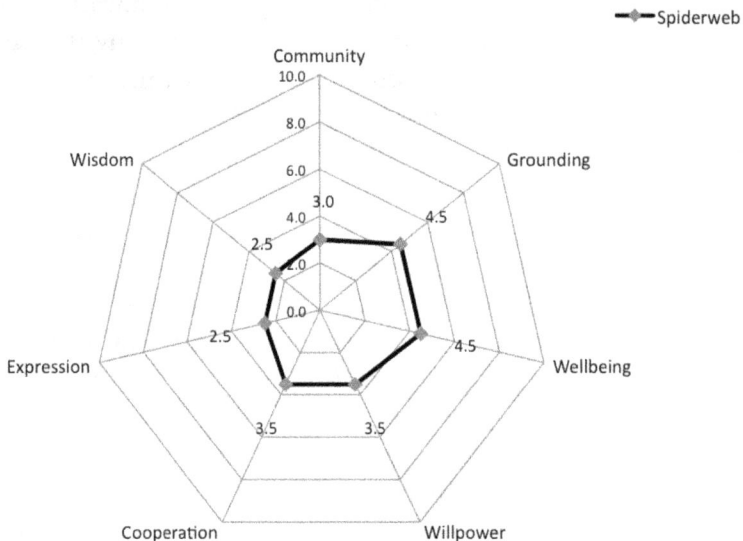

Figure 4.12

This image of the Organizational Energy System of Company B shows an organization where the energies are really closed, with evenly low assessments. It shows an overall state of deterioration and shortness of breath.

In general, unblocking some of the situations that anchor the energy system in this closed position will promptly bring a systemic improvement throughout the organization. That is, just by acting on a couple of critical points or axes, the whole system will easily improve in a clear and visible manner.

The points indicating greater blocking of the energy system in this company were lack of vision to deal with the uncertainty of a changing market (Wisdom), and insufficient communication both internally and towards the market (Expression). The Willpower axis also had a low assessment because the group felt that the organization did not live their corporate values genuinely.

Although the Cooperation axis did not get the lowest score, these were the most uneven assessments. When evaluating internal cooperation, a highly divergent reality emerged: there were cases where relationships between them were very good and others where relationships were cold and based on mistrust. The average rating of the axis does not show the difficult situations the management team was experiencing. There was an internal division. This could actually be seen in the assessments of the angles and the conversations that took place. Despite the fact that being able to talk about this openly was already a major improvement, it became clear that more action was needed in this regard.

When assessing the Cooperation axis for external cooperation, especially with customers, it was found that although the people serving customers directly did have a genuine cooperation will, the organization as a system did not have the ability to cooperate well with them. This was mainly due to the lack of flexibility of the organization (slow and rigid processes, systems and decision making) and the lack of cooperation between those who could create this flexibility.

Our job was to provide the conditions to generate a space for collaboration between managers and their departments. Thus, during the *Strategy* Phase, a system of shared mission, vision and values was developed. In order to clear uncertainties, the business environment and the ownership relationships were established, and common management objectives that were above personal differences were defined. Besides, executive accompanying processes (*coaching*) were started with some people who were certainly helpful.

From the beginning, we could see that the team began to soften internal tensions and to integrate their differences. They were willing to hold honest conversations. Both the CEO and the implementation team were able to see the changes when facing small everyday challenges and in the personal attitude of the management team in view of the upcoming change process.

Public agency

Organization C is an agency dependent of the government, with 15,000 employees dedicated to public assistance and social service.

At the initial stage of the process with Pinea3 methodology, this organization was in a stalemate that had been going for years and under strong external pressure. These two factors could eventually make the agency not fulfill their mission and become obsolete and dysfunctional in the near future. In turn, all this was already detrimental to the motivation of senior managers. Despite keeping their convictions, daily performance made them feel that the boat they were sailing was adrift. Other workers also felt discouraged by the same sense of drift and external pressures.

After a period of change, the new political and executive leaders were certain that they needed to act decisively. Working with Pinea3 methodology emerged as a valuable support throughout this process. The process should be carried out by introducing new elements, using reflection and implementation plans not previously used in the organization. In this way they wanted to provide a lever to rethink and reorganize the agency in harmony with new and future requirements. On the other hand, the process could be traumatic and efforts were needed to counter this effect. The adoption of this methodology helped to redirect or avoid conflicts.

THE PINEA3 METHODOLOGY®

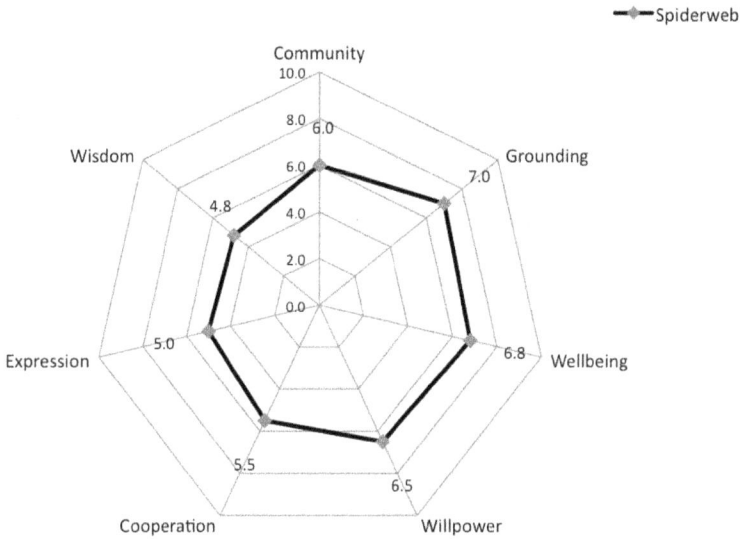

Figure 4.13

The diagnosis of this organization through its Energy System reflects a chart with a fairly regular profile. That is, without significant variations between the assessments. This often means that the organization is balanced, although it does not guarantee that this balance is always in a position where the energies flow well. When this happens, it is advisable to analyze the assessments of the different angles, as there is usually a lot of information in uneven ratings, which are hidden behind the average ratings of the axis.

The lowest ratings were 4.8 in the Wisdom axis, 5 in the Expression axis and 5.5 in the Cooperation axis. The ratings of the angles indicated more clearly the points where the organization was blocked and would not allow energy to flow throughout the system. These were, above all, the lack of a shared vision about the future of the organization and how to reach one. Although it was a highly efficient organization in their performance, they had lost their way and their strategic direction. On a more operational level, the bottlenecks were also internal cooperation with other public agencies, internal communication flowing only downwards as formal communication and the rigidity of internal processes and decision making. The senior management group quickly agreed that these were the key points to work with.

We began facilitating the development of a vision, mission and values system, which were the basis for initiating a thorough debate on the model needed to meet the challenges of the next decade. After that, the organization faced a restructuring process with strength and motivation. In this way, the necessary elements for an organization of this size to be set in motion were activated. The humanist approach of the methodology provided support to managers, not only to accept the changes coming from above, but also to help them bring about other necessary changes for the company to better fulfill its mission.

PART V

THE MRW CASE

- A Brief History of the Company
- Situation and Challenges in December 2011
- Working with Pinea3 – Discovery Phase
- Results of the OES Diagnosis
- Working with Pinea3 – Strategy Phase
- Learning and Reflections on Pinea3's Work
- Next Steps

We have chosen to end this book with a more complete case to illustrate that beyond the theoretical discourse that may sound vague and difficult to materialize, there is a real application to improve organizational health and prosperity.

MRW is a company that has already been chosen as a reference for different business cases that are used in the most prestigious business schools in Spain. To Pinea3, MRW is not only a company we are working with, implementing our transformational change methodology, but a real example of a company that has long operated in the new paradigm.

We have much to learn from this family business with a quiet leadership that has become a leading company nationwide and that is likely to become a referent worldwide in the coming years. MRW is the living proof that a focus on the people always ends up compensating other strategies that try to use them as "human resources". In his book "El primer café de la mañana, Reflexiones de un empresario" ("The first morning coffee, Reflections of an entrepreneur") [82], first published in 2007, Francisco Martín Frías already talked about the importance of becoming entrepreneurs that think on the triple bottom line.

As Francisco stated, "as business leaders, we must be prepared to devote time and energy to explain to shareholders why seemingly unrelated concepts such as profitability and social development are not only not incompatible, but can bring us many benefits when taken together." He also commented in this regard: "It is obvious (...) that the more profitable a company is, the more resources will be available to invest in social actions, and since 1993 MRW has assigned more than 1% of its turnover to such actions, clearly making MRW a more competitive company." Let us hope more entrepreneurs think this way. If you still have not read it, we recommend this little book full of interesting reflections on MRW and entrepreneurship in general. In any case here we make a short introduction of the company to set the case in context.

A Brief History of the Company

MRW, which dates back to 1977, was founded as a door to door courier in the city of Barcelona with the peculiarity that the messengers communicated with the central office through radiofrequency devices. Its founders were three advertisers who failed to manage operational growth. The company took heavy losses and was sold two years later. Thus, Francisco Martín Frías, a self-made entrepreneur, joined the company in 1979 along with two other investors and re-founded what would become a successful company. He made significant staff changes and took charge bringing in the simple and efficient leadership that characterizes him. MRW began to grow with the added value of being a fast and reliable courier company.

The original company was called Mensajeros Radio and it was not until 1988 that they changed the company name to MRW, adding the term Worldwide to reflect its international vocation. Since its inception Francisco, driven by a great business sense and, as he says, acting somewhat intuitively [82], created a company with a strong commitment to people and the environment in which it operated. With this spirit, Francisco expanded the company to take more than 10,000 employees in 2008, including direct employees and franchisees.

In the same year, Francisco had another visionary idea. He started his succession at the right time, promoting his son Francisco (Paco) Martin Villanueva, Paco from now on, to managing director and he assumed the role of the president. Half of the family businesses disappear in their attempt to allow the generational relay, and although there are no magic formulas, one of the most common mistakes is failing to truly delegate responsibilities to the heirs. In this case we found that the transfer was carried out thoughtfully.

With the occasion of the generational relay, part of the management team along with the father and son traveled throughout Spain in their first semester of work, visiting as many franchises as possible; another example of this human aspect that characterizes the MRW management style.

In the beginning of 2012, MRW was a national benchmark of social sustainability and new paradigm leadership. Many colleagues of the management team had participated in 116 conferences and presentations at various events in 2011 alone. At the end of 2011, MRW accumulated 212 awards from different Spanish and European institutions. In his book, Francisco Martín Frías spoke of the influence of luck on his project. We do not believe in luck, instead, we think this is created with our attitude. Nor do we believe in coincidence, but in causality; everything happens because we have done or thought something that motivates, triggers or causes it.

From 2008 until late 2011, Paco worked to transform a company that was tailored-made to his father into a professionalized company that had to cope with the new challenges. Paco explains it in his own words:

"When I took on the role of General Manager of the company, after more than 30 years of successful leadership by my father, I fell into a state of reflection and caution that would not last long, since the economic crisis in Spain was becoming more evident and the need to make decisions, often quick, difficult, brave and important, started to be urgent.

In recent months we had worked on a Strategic Plan for the company 2009-2011, so "part of the homework" had already been done. We started working in three very clear directions: the first was to direct the company towards greater customer focus, as we had overlooked this aspect for a long time. Thus, we created a sales network of our own, a marketing department, and a concern for sales improving our portfolio of services, while working to instill that mindset in the franchisees that was inexistent before and that we had not needed either. We know that in order to succeed we need the active participation of franchisees. Joining forces and having a clear horizon greatly helps us to be aligned in the project.

Secondly, we started to direct the organization towards internationalization. We had been operating In Portugal and Venezuela for more than twenty years, but now we started working "jointly". Until then, each geography had been working independently. Finally, we focused on the "professionalization" of the company. We concentrated on improving processes and systems, managing with a greater focus on efficiency, and improving and adapting the individuals' employability.

These were our targeted priorities. They were not few. A challenging relay (due to the success of my predecessor), a rampant economic crisis and an internal process improvement forced us to reinvent ourselves. It was a scenario of absolute uncertainty, where companies were disappearing day by day as a result of the drop in sales, in addition to the progressive implementation of technology in companies, which also entailed a decline in the volume of shipments. Of course we had to react, and the time to do so was limited..."

Situation and challenges in December 2011

In late 2011, in the midst of the Spanish, European and worldwide crisis, there were conflicting signs about the state of the company. On the one hand, the company ended 2011 with a growth volume of 9.3 %, when the sector registered a decline of 3% in the same year. It also consolidated its leadership in the courier industry and continued to attract talent for its focus on people. On the other hand, the economic results were still not the ones expected after two years of losses and so the situation had to be reversed. In December 2011 there were a number of challenges that the company had to face in the coming years. In the words of Paco Martin, they had to:

- *"Consolidate an economic turnaround emerging from a period of decline in turnover and profitability in the two previous years. And all this amidst a period of strong economic and social instability.*

- *Transform a business model focused on parcel delivery to businesses (B2B), to adopt a mixed approach with a greater focus on individuals (B2C and C2C).*
- *Incorporate into our operational management some routes that were not supervised and that in some cases threatened the competitiveness of our services due to the highly uneven fares.*
- *Strive towards internationalization.*
- *Remain a leader in social sustainability and become a leader also in environmental sustainability in the future.*
- *Consolidate changes in systems, processes and team management (professionalization, employability, focus on results...).*
- *Consolidate an organization focused on efficiency and austerity.*
- *Consolidate a network of franchises that after the expansion in recent years was folding back and optimizing.*
- *Complete and make large technological investments profitable.*
- *Develop a continuity project starting our second strategic cycle 2012-2014 (formerly 2009-2011).*
- *We were forced to transform the organization into a business model oriented to high volume and not to marginality, as we would have wanted to remain. But the market forced us to do so."*

Besides the explicit business challenges, in all family businesses there are, by definition, other hidden challenges that should also be treated as they have an effect on the "organizational energy body" and thus on the prosperity of the company. These companies, for example, coexist with two energy systems, the organizational and the family one, which often interfere with each other. The family hierarchy is not necessarily reproduced in the organization and this can lead to tensions that cannot be solved rationally, as they are essentially emotional conflicts. These are irrational by nature and can only be solved from the heart. In the case of MRW, we find Francisco, president, founder and father; Esther Martin, corporate director of CSR and director of the MRW Foundation *"Red de Emociones"*, and eldest daughter; and Paco, CEO and youngest son. Being aware of this and taking it into account in our work with the team and the organization are important success factors.

Working with Pinea3 - Discovery Phase

In Part IV of the book we have described the general lines of the transformational methodology proposed by Pinea3. In this section, we will briefly explain the work we did with MRW including some occasional anecdotes of this process.

Kick-off Workshop:

The *kick-off*, is a key meeting in which the participation of all team members is important. MRW was organized in a matrix organization of 14 people where a large number of executives lived in Barcelona. The company only had international presence in Portugal and Venezuela. In the end, the representative of Venezuela did not attend the meeting in person but connected via telephone. It was important to "be energetically present" and in this way we could have him present somehow in that initial *kick-off* meeting.

The objective of this workshop was to present the Pinea3 work methodology and the process roadmap. The workshop also included some creative work to explore the MRW concept of prosperity using the right side of the brain.

At the end of the *kick-off* meeting, one of the participants told us that he was a bit skeptical about all this and that he could not clearly see the connection between what we did and the bottom line of MRW. One may think that it is not the best remark you can receive during the initial meeting of a project with a client, but it is actually a great opportunity, and it emerged spontaneously thanks to the culture of dialogue and openness in the company. There were several ways to answer this question. The most obvious was trying to convince with logical arguments and examples that our work would positively impact the bottom line indeed, but not immediately. We could have mentioned as well the business indicators scientifically measuring the change in the organization. But all this would have been a cognitive response overlooking the emotions that person felt at the moment. On that occasion, we appreciated his comment for having raised a doubt that was in the system and we took the opportunity to integrate it into the process. After a while the answer became clear for that person.

Exploration Workshop:

This workshop uses the latest tools that have been developed in the market to work with teams and organizations. The systemic constellations or configurations are, as noted in Part II of the book, a technique born in Germany in the 90s based on works with family systems and very recently introduced in organizations. It is a way of helping to realize existing blockages in a system, whether a family, an organization or a project. This method of bringing up hidden issues has gained much acceptance in Germany and has started to spread widely throughout Europe. Through the human representation of scenarios and problem situations, the persons involved can see that the initial interpretation of the issue discussed may be incomplete or wrong. Thus, it helps to rethink assumptions and to have an open mind to see new solutions.

The systemic configurations are designed so that a person (or a few at most) can analyze a situation or problem falling within their remit by making a few key questions. When this technique is applied to an organization, the owner or the chief executive are the ones who must make these strategic questions. Paco, as CEO, chose the topics, along with the facilitator (also referred to as "constellator"). The workshop was also attended by José Miguel Valenzuela (Deputy CEO), Esther Martin (CSR corporate director), and Silvia Vílchez (corporate director of people and organization). The workshop explored two important issues: one was the new *e-commerce* strategy of the company where they ratified the importance of having a shared vision with the franchises on this issue. The other was the configuration of the global health status of the MRW system through the seven energy or prosperity axes. Reading these human configurations is always relevant if we are open to receive answers to their questions.

Awareness Workshop

The *Awareness* workshop closes the first phase (*Discovery*) and starts the second (*Strategy*). As we said before, the main objective of this final stage workshop is to agree on the business diagnosis based on its energy system (OES). It is a self-diagnosis and so our role in this dynamic is to act as facilitators of the awareness process of the group. To this aim, we use several techniques and the philosophy on which *coaching* is built: You cannot teach anyone who does not want to learn, or say anything to anyone who does not want to hear. It is much more effective to question and motivate learning. Thus, we conducted the meeting with all the executives of the first phase (14 people in the case of MRW). It is important that all the voices in the system are heard and that not only a few, usually the most senior, monopolize the result.

Regardless of their degree of evolution, all organizations have areas of improvement and dark areas that went unnoticed or were ignored in the past for whatever reason. That is why in all the processes we have always facilitated there is so much to learn. MRW is actually one of the companies with a higher level of consciousness from those we have worked for. A higher consciousness outwards will motivate the work on social and environmental responsibility. A consciousness oriented inwards will focus on our employees and collaborators and will develop an attitude of genuine listening and learning. That is what allowed the MRW management team to start a dialogue on "pending conversations" that other companies would have been uneasy about. We know from experience that tensions that are more or less hidden can emerge in any system and that an effective way to bring them out is to explore those "pending conversations". These conversations may not come up easily at the right time and are set aside, but it is important to deal with them occasionally. Only the most forward-thinking executives are opened to these dynamics.

After completing the first phase, Silvia, human resource director, addressed us with a noble concern and she made a point that we would like to share here. She asked us if the work we were doing was congruent with the fact that the company, like most of the Spanish society at that time, focused solely on economic viability. Silvia told us:"We will have to do without a number of people and perhaps it is best to leave the work with Pinea3 until this process has finished." We said that in our opinion the work we were doing was not only perfectly compatible, but it helped to bring awareness on how this downsizing process would take place. If it is necessary to reduce the staff to ensure the viability of a long-term project, it is something unwanted but it has to be addressed as soon as possible. It is like cutting the branch of a tree; it is best not to wait if we know we will have to cut it anyway. If the company focuses temporarily on the "P" for *Profit* (economic aspect), leaving aside the "P"s for *People* and *Planet* (social and environmental aspects), it is not a bad thing. It is a matter of priorities; it can be compared to a situation where someone has to fight a disease and spends a week in hospital or resting at home and thus has to neglect physical exercise or his social contribution, for example. But it was a rightful concern: if it had been a change of corporate values (in a company that had always been an example socially) and that from that point on they only wanted to make money, there would definitely have been a conflict with the work we were doing with the group. As this was not the case, we continued with our accompaniment work to support the process of change and growth in MRW, possibly bringing light as well to the process of staff termination.

Results of the OES Diagnosis

The result of the first phase is a self-diagnosis of the degree of prosperity of the company. This self-diagnosis, which is agreed by the entire management team, reflects the health status of the organizational energy body. In Figure 5.1 we show the graph resulting from the assessments with MRW.

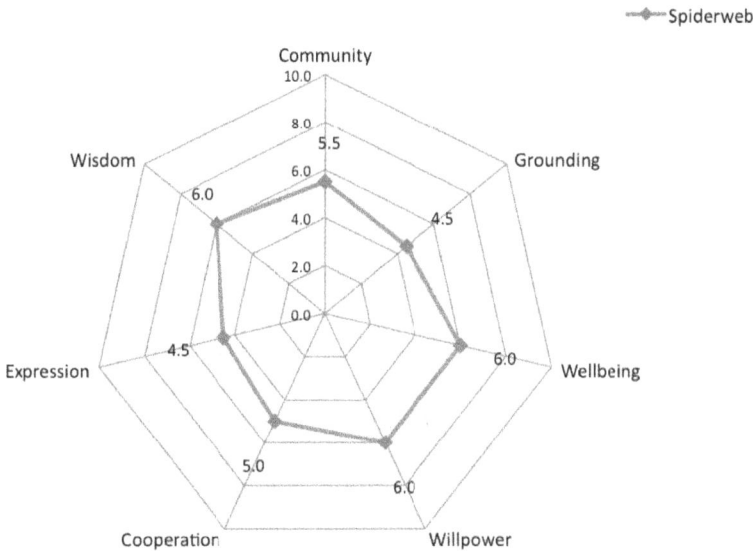

Figure 5.1

The middle global rating of the OES is 5 points out of 10. This is a way of assessing the business prosperity of the organizational energy body that is being analyzed. However, it is important to emphasize that the purpose of this self-diagnosis is to agree on a reality from an internal point of view that focuses on improvement, which is why the ratings tend to be critical. The results are not intended to be compared with any other graphic of any other company. In fact, the assessment methodology we follow does not pursue an objective approach with a scientific method. Quite the contrary, we wanted to use a subjective approach that the management team could use to realize the areas for improvement that limit the system prosperity. Similarly to what happens at an individual level (e.g. in leadership development), when an assessment is accepted by the self, our resources are focused on improvement. And this is our goal.

We will now capture some of the most relevant comments that came out in the work with the MRW management team. This will demonstrate, once again, the applicability of the concept of the Organizational Energy System (OES)® in a real case and to better understand the three angles of each of the seven Organizational Chakras:

Grounding:

The first axis or Grounding chakra is composed, as we saw in Part III, of the following three angles: foundational energy, added value and available resources.

The foundational energy was rated with a 4 by the MRW executive team. On the positive side, they valued the fact that after 34 years of history, the person who was practically the founder, Francisco Martín Frías, still had an active position in the company as President. In terms of improvement areas, the group highlighted the fact that with the recent growth and the recent generational change, much of that vital foundational energy had not been passed on to new generations.

For the first time, they raised the issue of whether the MRW system should be assessed with or without their franchises, which are independent business units and legal companies. It is very important for our work with organizations to define exactly the Organizational Energy body we are working with: what is inside and what is outside? The incorporation of more than 1,300 franchises (employing more than 10,000 people) was one of the reasons why the group decided to choose a negative rating for the presence of that foundational energy in the MRW staff and collaborators, an angle that would have had a higher mark otherwise.

The second angle of the Grounding chakra is the added value the company brings to the market and therefore the fertility it finds in it, which was valued with a 6. Since MRW was in transition: from a courier company focused on the professional market (B2B), to a leading transport company in the e-commerce business model (B2C and C2C), we assessed globally the value that it provided to the market. While there still was room for improvement (4 points), the team appreciated the contribution of added value to the current market. The value we bring to the market should not be mistaken with our market share, although there is probably a correlation between the two. We can have a very large percentage of the market because in the past we were contributing with a high value. However, it is important to assess critically the real value we contribute today. An interesting indicator, for example, is to ask whether our market share is increasing or decreasing compared to the competition.

The third and last angle of the first axis evaluates the resources available to the company. The mark was 3.5, as they considered that despite being in a good situation, especially compared to the competition, the boom years of the past were gone and there was a lot of pressure on pricing. Another appreciation was the fact that many of the employees had to progressively adapt their skills to fit the resulting MRW after the strategic transformation. The average rating also reflected the global crisis and, consequently, that there was a lot of room for improvement in the availability of resources.

Wellbeing:

The second axis or Wellbeing chakra is composed by the three following angles: emotions, adaptability to change and brand image.

Emotions, or the level of emotional comfort, were assessed with a 4.5. There was an interesting discussion about the difference between the well-being of workers in the central offices and that of franchises, which highlighted the lack of knowledge or attention that the Head Quarter sometimes paid to their franchisees.

Adaptability to change was assessed with a 5, though there were uneven positions, especially regarding the adaptability of individual contributors and managers. They also talked about certain inflexibility of the company's processes and hence this average mark.

The brand image was valued with a 7.5. This high mark was due to a good image of MRW in the marketplace. The company had been doing things very well for years with a focus on people and therefore it was recognized by the market. The mark was not higher because MRW was known and recognized in the B2B, but not yet in the B2C and C2C, and so there was still room for improvement.

Willpower:

The third axis or Willpower chakra is composed of the three following perspectives: mission / purpose, values and power.

All the angles of this chakra were measured with an average of 6, reflecting positive aspects of the organization but, at the same time, a clear area for improvement. The purpose/mission of the company and its values were recently revised and although they lacked clarity and diffusion, the team felt they were representative of MRW at the moment.

Power and how it is exercised (control vs. delegation) was also an aspect that did not stand out either as negative or positive in MRW management. It was somehow related to the previous comment on rigid processes that sometimes did not facilitate *empowerment*.

Cooperation:

The fourth axis consists on cooperation with external partners, internal cooperation and relationship with customers.

External cooperation was assessed with a 5, considering that the company worked well enough with their environment, even if it was not one of its strongest points. Since MRW was a very vertically integrated company in their operations, they did not frequently use suppliers and strategic partners and this angle was not given too much weight or importance in the discussion.

Internal cooperation was assessed with a 6 and the good atmosphere of collaboration was considered one of the strong points of the company. The mark was not higher because trust could be better in some cases and departments. It reflected that in order for this energy to flow better, they should somehow encourage more authentic cooperation throughout the organization and across hierarchical levels.

Customer relationship was assessed with a 4. This assessment was low because it included more than 1,300 franchises in this category and they considered they were not doing a good job in collaborating with them. It has been important here to have the participation of three representatives to have their voice heard in the complete MRW system.

THE MRW CASE

Expression:

The fifth axis or Expression chakra is composed of the angles of external communication, internal bottom-up and horizontal communication, and internal top-down communication.

External communication was valued with a 4.5 to show that there was a clear area for improvement in this regard. It was mentioned that MRW had been a "quiet leader", especially regarding their policies with people, and that they had been "discovered" by the market. Maybe it was time to capitalize on all they did well, communicating it better, especially for a strong entry into transportation of consumer goods.

The internal upward and horizontal communication was the lowest mark of this chakra. It was given a 4 because it was still hard to listen to each other, especially bottom-up. In the past there had been a stronger hierarchical structure and there were still remnants of that energy that needed to be cleared. The poor upward communication between franchisees and central offices also influenced this assessment.

Internal downward communication was valued with a 5 as it was one of those things the company did well but could do better. The mark was lowered again considering that this downward communication did not reach the franchises as it should.

Wisdom:

The sixth axis or Wisdom chakra is composed of the three angles of knowledge management, strategic vision and decision making.

Knowledge management in MRW was assessed with a 5. As it was an operations company there were many documents and processes, but these were often not user-friendly and were not helpful for the user. Thus, the way knowledge was managed, including the acquisition of external knowledge, had an average energy.

The strategic vision obtained a consensual mark of 6. Here there was much discussion as the company was in a strategic review process where the vision and strategic plan had been reviewed recently. The vision of the past three years was clear, inspiring and fairly shared, but the new cycle was not finished yet and had still had not been communicated. Thus, there were requests in the system asking for clarity on the company's strategy for the next three years.

Decision making was also valued as a strong point of the company with a 6.5. In these self-evaluation processes teams are often critical of themselves. This score indicates that the group felt the company had good strategic decision making processes, but also talked about possible improvements by managing important decisions faster whenever they were blocked for some reason.

Community:

The seventh axis or Community chakra has the following components: organizational development, social and environmental consciousness, and systemic understanding.

Organizational development was assessed with a 5.5. MRW was a company that had always believed in people and somehow there was willingness towards continuous learning and organizational development. What lowered a higher mark in this angle was the understanding that they still had not completed the transition from small family business to a fully professionalized enterprise where organizational and professional development was an integral part of the company. Here, once again, the voices of the franchises could be heard as they often seemed to live in a world apart.

Social and environmental consciousness was certainly one of the strengths of MRW and was rated with a 6.5. The reason why this mark was not even higher was the component of environmental responsibility. As a transportation company, they had a big impact on the average CO_2 emissions to the atmosphere, and it was considered an area that could be improved in the future.

Systemic understanding was valued with a 5. This is always a difficult angle to value for teams, as it is still a very new concept for entrepreneurs and executives. The team, though, clearly understood the concept of the company as a living system and acknowledged that they still had a long way to go to develop its full potential and incorporate it into their daily management.

Working with Pinea3 - Strategy Phase

After realizing what can be done to improve the organizational prosperity and performance, we must get down to work to create an action plan, both realistic and engaging. Most companies already have a strategic plan of some kind and the challenge here is always the same: to integrate and improve the plan, typically more *hard* (business) component, with its more *soft* (humanistic) component. Integrating the "What" with the "How", including not only economic indicators but also indicators measuring the health of the organization, adopting a more comprehensive and holistic vision of the system.

As we explained earlier, this phase develops what we call the Organizational Prosperity Plan (OPP) as a direct result of the work in the first phase. Therefore, the OPP must be integrated with the current strategic plan reflecting the business objective of the company to make a new improved plan.

Extension Workshop:

This workshop aims to enlarge the team of internal transformational agents, from the original team to an extended team. During a day and a half workshop we worked with 23 people who were added to the original team in the process of change that was underway. The election of the members to become part of the extended team is usually done by asking each of the managers in the initial group to appoint one or two people from their teams to join the process. In this case, they decided to expand the group throughout the seven departments with greater weight and/or a greater number of staff: Logistics, Operations, Spain, Portugal, International, Finance and, the novelty, also Franchises. They chose not to include the region of Venezuela because they had a very different reality compared to the Iberian Peninsula. They decided spontaneously that the energy system being evaluated was the Iberian Peninsula, leaving Venezuela outside that work.

It was the first time in the history of MRW that franchisees were invited to participate in one of these workshops or conferences. The very decision of including the franchisees as part of the system already provided a different level of consciousness, as we saw in the previous chapter. Thus, three people were invited representing that community: one representing the large franchises with a higher turnover, another representing medium franchises and the third representing the smallest.

Just like the original team of managers, they were all satisfied with the teamwork and the management initiative to undertake this organizational improvement process, which also went down a hierarchical level and took them into consideration. Many commented on the importance of creating cross-organizational spaces for dialogue in the company with heterogeneous groups that would certainly help co-create their new reality together.

Integration Workshop:

In the two previous workshops (*Self-Awareness* and *Extension*) both teams created a separate list of ideas in a brainstorming session on how to improve the prosperity of the company based on its self-diagnosis. After this divergent work, this workshop (*Integration*), is where convergence starts by grouping the ideas that are more aligned with the business strategy and the present reality. As Ferrer Arpí and Ponti [83] highlight, a good idea that is not applicable can be very creative but does not necessarily bring innovation to the system. The aim of the organization is to implement these creative ideas, making them a constant innovation engine. After a creative divergence phase comes a rationalization and prioritization phase to assess those useful aspects and ideas, in this case for the process of improving the strategic plan.

The *Integration* workshop lasted one and a half days, like most, as this was the middle point to keep a transformation process alive with minimum effort and investment. This workshop was the first time that both teams were together, creating the extended team of internal change agents. For MRW they were the 14 original management team members plus 23 additional people who started with the Extension Team, a total of 38 people.

They were all happy to share this space: some participants commented that it was "a luxury" to work outside the office on strategic issues such as these on a cross-organizational basis and without rigid hierarchies. Group dynamics also contributed to create a more horizontal and relaxed climate that helped to improve the existing strategic plan.

Commitment Workshop:

This workshop closes the second phase (*Strategy*) and opens the third (*Realization*). As we have described above, it is the workshop where the Organizational Prosperity Plan (OPP) ends and where the team commits to comply with it. It was also a one day and a half workshop with the extended team (38 people).

The leaders of each strategic line presented their plan to the rest of the team and elaborated how they were going to improve it based on the input from the work done with Pinea3. The most common issues were a focus on better communication at all levels and better cooperation with franchises, which had to be more integrated into the system from now on.

In this workshop, we decided to incorporate a *beat* of *Listening and Feedback* to illustrate the format of the *beats* in the third stage of the methodology. This was also intended so that this team could benefit from something as important and underdeveloped in MRW as good listening and feedback.

Learning and Reflections on Pinea3's work

In the words of Paco Martín Villanueva: *"As I write these lines the work with Pinea3 is not over.... so I do not have the time perspective nor the actual feedback of the rest of the team, that is for me very important.*

Having worked on this project with Pinea3 has allowed us many things, all of them positive. I will try to explain them but certainly I cannot do it in order of priority. On the one hand, it has allowed us to work, talk and prioritize the message People (for People, Planet, Profit). The crisis, the generational relay, the environment, the shift in the business... could be sending a message to the organization regarding values that were different from the original and desired ones. Working on this project has enabled us to transmit to the management team that the "how" is as important as the "what".

We have been able to explore, through a completely different methodology, systemic aspects of the organization and its performance, so our integral vision has grown and evolved.

Furthermore, we have shared so much time together with people we work with, but with whom we do not always have a "moment of serenity and reflection". We have been able to do it at a time when the company is undergoing a very important turning point.

Likewise, in these sessions we have communicated, worked and internalized strategy. They have helped us to strengthen organizational priorities within the team that will enable their development.

We have grown in human and cultural aspects, as the methodology used has connected us with experiences that we would not have encountered otherwise (the world of mandalas, conscious nutrition, yoga, music,...).

We believe that these workshops have made us different: better, more human, more aware, more cautious, more systemic. Our attitude when facing transformation is a key starting point. The companies of the future are those with a greater ability to adapt to the environment. We must become aware that leaders in organizations are those that act as change agents and who are constantly able to interpret, design and transform.

We must not forget that organizations are living systems in constant motion. Now, the important thing is how these movements lead us to excellence. It is therefore essential that the whole system aligns around a clear direction.

This methodology is available to any organization. However, it must come from the willingness to participate in a group where the roles/positions are left at the door. It is essential to participate as peer team members. For those who manage large teams it is positive to hear directly good things from your people, but it is also very healthy to listen to the bad ones. It is precisely in the areas of improvement where we should focus on and take action. That awareness is a leverage point that is available to any manager, however, you will need to create the mechanisms to activate it.

At MRW we have always been known for doing things differently, of course the work with Pinea3 is extraordinary, as it is not some kind of training, but the aim is to acquire a higher level of consciousness and nothing else.

It is exciting to involve and engage the team to improve the scores received on the 7 axes. Hence, there will be future sessions to analyze ourselves again and see how we have evolved. But certainly that level of demand is for the whole team as all of them are the leaders needed to progress and transform the organization to make it last in time."

Next Steps

The *Realization* phase, as we explained above, is designed to suit each organization. We know from experience that in order to carry out a cultural transformation or a successful business improvement process, it is necessary to adapt to each situation. Thus, this phase adapts its intensity to the reality of the company. We saw the concept of intensity in the theoretical explanation of this phase and the fact that it must find a balance between the magnitude of change, the urgency and the resources. The magnitude of the desired change indicates whether the change is smaller or larger, the urgency will determine the need to achieve that change in time, and the resources available can speed up or slow down the implementation time. In fact, the urgency, along with the resources, will determine the final priority we can give to the transformation process and its timing.

In this phase, we also need to take into account that the final transformation of an organization will not occur unless the supporting systems and processes also change. The organization changes if the attitudes and behaviors of employees change. And they will be able to maintain these changes over time more easily if they develop new incentives from a new structure. If a person with alcohol problems joins a sports program, s/he will have an incentive to stop drinking and improve fitness through sport, instead of wasting his time at the bar. Likewise, we ought to change those outdated structures and thought paradigms in organizations that could trigger some unwanted behavior.

In line with this, it is important to emphasize the influence of *role models* in any change process. The owners of the company, the general management and the senior executives have an important role in the improvement process and the organizational transformation. They must keep promoting this change and leading by example. They are internal change agents that should continue motivating that change every day.

As discussed above, organizational development, like human development, occurs in a spiral motion. It is not, as perhaps we would like, a linear process upwards. This means that sometimes there might be setbacks, like when you learn a new language. It is perseverance and determination in our efforts that will eventually lead to success.

We mentioned before that it is important to measure change and improvement somehow. And we should remember that even if we work with *soft* indicators, it is possible to assess the evolution scientifically. Therefore, we have developed a method that measures the actual improvement in the company from the global perspective provided by the Organizational Energy System (OES)®. The start of the *Realization* phase is the right time to distribute the P7Assessment® questionnaire among the interest groups that are to be considered for this assessment: employees (multiple levels, countries and divisions), and external partners such as suppliers, customers, and even society, if desired. This questionnaire gathers information from all those stakeholders on the status of the company, its image and the emotions it generates. It is similar to the analysis process followed by management in the *Discovery* phase but now the "photo" is composed of a 360-degree view of the company. It is therefore a much more objective and it is re-evaluated after some time, depending on the transformational objectives of each particular project. As we said before, this is the most scientific method to measure a real organizational change according to the seven variables that all the improvement work is based on.

We are satisfied with the evolution we have seen in MRW, a company with a clear positioning as a conscious leader, and we want to thank Paco Martín Valenzuela and his management team for their courage in undertaking this process of organizational improvement. In late March 2012, when we first published this book in Spanish, MRW was at the beginning of the *Realization* phase and we had to wait some time to evaluate their actual performance. It is like many Hollywood blockbuster movies, there is always a second part.

ACKNOWLEDGEMENTS

Gratitude is one of the basic principles of the universe. It is important to acknowledge those who have helped us along the way.

We would like to start thanking our clients for their trust and for giving us the opportunity to develop this methodology and the chance to implement our mission and purpose. In particular, thanks to Joan Cañellas for his conscious leadership and for being the first who hired us to work with his organization, in Spain and recently in the USA.

In this second edition we want to acknowledge and thank Francesca Gabetti and Erika Uffindell, our two new partners at Pinea3, for helping us maintain Pinea3 project alive and with renewed energy.

We want to thank everybody who have given us valuable input to make this book more coherent and enjoyable for a broad audience: Silvia Vilchez, Giuseppe Cavallo and Manel Balet for the first edition and Wayne Hart, Kevin O'Gorman, George Houston, and Chris Watz from CCL for this current edition.

We want to thank as well all Pinea3 collaborators for supporting us and making our work possible all these years. To our important collaborators: Angélica Morales, Jaime Ripoll, Oscar Guirado, Joan Corbalán, Fabian Frutos, Anna Alcayde, Kelly Simmons, Carlos Surroca, Victor Angel, Maria Rosa Plans, Manel Balet, Eliane Bernard, Francesca Gabetti, Giuseppe Cavallo, Trini Rodriguez, and Eva Miletorp. And to our friends and personal healers who helped us to stay focused and resourceful: Viviana, Victor and Arnauld.

This work would not have been possible without the support of our families. So thanks to our partners, sons and daughters for their unconditional support and their patience: Kelly, Glòria, Anna, Mateu, Ian, Mariona, Marc, Jan, Rita and Guim.

Thank you all from the bottom of our hearts!

ENRIC, JOAN AND XAVIER

REFERENCES

1. Hamel, G., *The Future of Management*. 2007, Boston, MA: Harvard Business School Press.
2. Lama, D., *The Universe in a Single Atom: The Convergence of Science and Spirituality*. 2005: Morgan Road Books.
3. Scharmer, O., *Theory U: Leading from the Future as It Emerges*. 2007, Cambridge, MA: Society for Organizational Learning.
4. WWF, *The NEW climate deal: A pocket guide*. 2009, World Wide Fund for Nature: Cambridge, UK.
5. Arpa, A., *Summer 2011*, in *Intermón Oxfam*. 2011.
6. *Survey of more than 400 people at the top 10% of society in 10 countries*. 2004, Center for media and democracy's sourcewatch.
7. ONU. http://www.un.org/es/globalcompact/principles.shtml.
8. Lozano, J.M. and M. Vilanova, *Una aposta anomenada sostenibilitat*, in *La Vanguardia*. 2011: Barcelona.
9. Hopkins, M.S., *Ocho razones por las que la sostenibilidad cambiará la gestión*, in *Harvard Deusto Business Review*. 2010: Barcelona.
10. Quinn, L. and J. Baltes, *Leadership and The Triple Bottom Line: Bringing Sustainability and Corporate Social Responsibility to Live* A CCL Research White Paper, 2007.
11. Thornton, G., *Corporate responsability: Burden or opportunity?*, in *Business Week Research Services*. 2007.
12. Choice, J., *CSR Reputation Effects on MBA* Stanford University, 2003.
13. Porter, M. and K. M., *Creating Shared Value*. Harvard Business Review, 2011.
14. Schumacher, E.F., *Buddist Economics*, in *Small Is Beautiful: Economics as if People Mattered*, E.F. Schumacher, Editor. 1973.
15. O'Toole, J. and W. Bennis, *A Culture of Candor*. Harvard Business Review, 2009.
16. Felber, C., *Neue Werte für die Wirtschaft. Eine Alternative zu und Kommunismus Kapitalismus*. 2008, Vienna: Deuticke publishing house.
17. Trompenaars, F. and P. Ten Hoopen, *The Enlightened Leader: An introduction to the chakras of leadership*. 2009: Jossey-Bass.

18. www.consciousleadershipconnection.com.

19. www.consciouscapitalism.org.

20. www.wholeheartedleaders.com.

21. www.iamthedoc.com.

22. Bhanoo, S.N., *How Meditation May Change the Brain*, in *New York Times*. 2011.

23. Woods, W., *Meditating at Work: A new Approach to Managing Overload*. Noetic Now Journal, 2012.

24. Levin, J., *How the universe got its spots*. 2002: Princeton University Press.

25. Chasse, M.V.B. and W. Arntz, *¿¡Y tu que sabes II!? ("What the bleep !? Down the rabbit hole?")* 2006, Captured Light Distribution.

26. Emoto, M., *Mensajes del agua (translated from: "Messagues in Water")*. 2003, Barcelona: La Liebre de Marzo.

27. Maruso, M., *Hay emociones que pueden matarte*, in *La Vanguardia (La Contra)*. 2008: Barcelona.

28. Chasse, M.V.B. and W. Arntz, *¿¡Y tu que sabes!? ("What the bleep do we know!?")*. 2006, Captured Light Distribution.

29. Cos, J. and X. Tarré, *Gestionar un equipo a través de su energía (Team Energy)*, in *Team Beat*, E. Bernal and J.V. Zoggel, Editors. 2011, EADA Centro de Innovación: Barcelona.

30. Senge, P., *La quinta disciplina (translated from: "The Fifth Discipline")*. 2005, Barcelona: Granica.

31. Simmons, K. and D. Hudnut, *El equipo como sistema: una nueva forma de entender su funcionamiento (Team System)*, in *Team Beat*, E. Bernal and J.V. Zoggel, Editors. 2011, EADA Centro de Innovación: Barcelona.

32. Mindell, A., *The Deep Democracy of Open Forums*. 2002, Charlottesville, VA: Hampton Roads Publishing Company Inc.

33. Stam, J.J., *Fields of Connection: The Practice of Organisational Constellations*. 2006.

34. Wilbert, K., *The Integral Vision*. 2007, Boston (MA): Shambhala Publications Inc.

35. Dispenza, J., *Evolve your brain: The science of changing your mind*. 2007, Deerfield Beach, FL: Health Communications, Inc.

36. Goleman, D., *Inteligencia Emocional (translated from: "Emotional Intelligence")*. 1996, Barcelona: Kairón.

37. Geus, A.d., *The Living Company*. 1997, Boston: Harvard Business School Press.

38. Barrett, R., *Liberating the Corporate Soul: Building a Visionary Organization*. 1998, Woburn, MA: Butterworth-Heinemann.

39. Guillory, W.A., *The Living Organization: Spirituality in the Workplace*. 2000, Salt Lake City, Utah: Innovations International Inc., Publishing Division.

40. Fowler, C.W., *Systemic Management: Sustainable Human Interactions with Ecosystems and the Biosphere*. 2009, Oxford: Oxford University Press.

41. Senge, P., *Foreword*, in *The Living Company*, A.d. Geus, Editor. 1997, Nicholas Brealey Publishing Limited: London, UK & Naperville (IL), USA.

42. Wilbert, K., *Integral Theory of Consciousness.* Journal of Consciousness Studies, 1997: p. 71-92.

43. Senge, P., *Leading Beyond The Walls.* 1999, San Francisco, CA Jossey-Bass Inc.

44. www.avaaz.org.

45. Secretan, L., *One: The art and practice of conscious leadership.* 2006, Caledon, Ontario, Canada: The Secretan Center Inc.

46. Kofman, F., *Metamanagement, La nueva con-ciencia de los negocios.* 2001, Buenos Aires: Ediciones Granica.

47. Kennedy, R., *Full original speach:* http://bit.ly/h8iqzH.

48. Wikipedia (napalm):. http://es.wikipedia.org/wiki/Napalm.

49. Schwartz, T. and C. McCarthy, *Manage Your Energy, Not Your Time*, in *Harvard Business Review.* 2007.

50. Blanchard, K., *Liderazgo de máximo nivel: la clave de una organización de alto rendimiento (translated from: "Leading at a Higher Level").* 2007, Barcelona: Granica.

51. Judith, A. and S. Vega, *The Sevenfold Journey, Reclaiming Mind, Body & Spirit Through the Chakras.* 1993, Berkeley, California, EUA: The Crossing Press.

52. Wauters, A., *The Book of Chakras.* 2002, London: Quarto Publishing plc.

53. Tuan, L., *El gran libro de los chakras, como activar los centros de la fuerza vital.* 2007, Barcelona: Editorial De Vecchi.

54. Brennan, B.A., *Manos que curan (translated from: "Hands of Light").* 2008, Madrid: Planeta.

55. Kim, W.C. and R. Mauborgne, *La estrategia del océano azul (translated from: "Blue Ocean Strategy").* 2005, Barcelona: Granica.

56. Bernal, E., *Colaborando en la diversidad (Team Diversity)*, in *Team Beat*, E. Bernal and J.V. Zoggel, Editors. 2011, EADA Centro de Innovación: Barcelona.

57. Morgado, I., *Emociones e inteligencia social.* 2007, Barcelona: Ariel.

58. Collins, J., *Good to Great: Why some companies make the leap... and others don't.* 2001, New York: HarperCollins Publications Inc.

59. *This vision/mission/purpose statement was taken from the Internet at the time of writing this book (2013). These statements may have changed at present but it still serves our intent well: to illustrate some real examples and comment about them.*

60. Blanchard, K., J. Carlos, and A. Randolph, *Las 3 claves para el empowerment (translated from "3 Keys to Empowerment").* 2001, Barcelona: Granica.

61. Charan, R., S. Drotter, and J. Noel, *The Leadership Pipeline: How to Build the Leadership Powered Company.* 2000, San Francisco, CA, USA: Jossey-Bass.

62. Virgili, P. and J. Wallowits, *La reconciliación con el consumidor.* 2011, Barcelona: Empresa Activa.

63. Anella, www.anella.cat.

64. McCauley, C., *Making Leadership Happen.* Center for Creative Leadership, 2011.

65. Rogers, P. and M. Blenko, *Who has the D? How Clear Decision Roles Enhance Organizational Performance.* Harvard Business Review, 2006.

66. Mintzberg, H. and F. Westley, *Decision Making: It's not what you think.* MIT SLOAN MANACEMENT REVIEW, 2001.

67. Adrià, F. www.elbullifoundation.org. April 2012].

68. Chesbrough, H., *Open Innovation, The New Imperative For Creating and Profiting from Technology.* 2003, Boston: Harvard Business School Publishing Corporation.

69. Time, T. http://www.time.com/time/world/article/0,8599,1987628,00.html.

70. www.medinge.org. April 2012].

71. www.aquamarinepower.com.

72. http://www.cajanavarra.es/es/home.htm.

73. www.masdarcity.ae/en/index.aspx.

74. www.theworldchallenge.co.uk.

75. www.ted.com.

76. Melé, J.A., *Dinero y conciencia, ¿A quién sirve mi dinero?* 2009, Barcelona: Plataforma Editorial.

77. Melé, J., *¿Dejas que tu dinero financie armas y contaminación?*, in *La Vanguardia (La Contra).* 2011: Barcelona.

78. McGuire, J., et al., *Transforming Your Organization.* Global Organizational Development White Paper, 2009.

79. Epstein, D.M., *The 12 stages of healing: A network approach to wholeness.* 1994, Novato, CA: Amber-Allen Publishing & New World Library.

80. Prochaska, J.O., J.C. Norcross, and C.C. Diclemente, *Changing for Good.* 2006, New York: Collins.

81. Beck, D.E. and C.C. Cowan, *Spiral Dynamics: Masterin Values, Leadership and Change.* 1996, Malden, MA: Blackwell Publishing Ltd.

82. Martín Frías, F., *El primer café de la mañana, Reflexiones de un empresario.* 2007, Barcelona: Gestión 2000.

83. Ferrer Arpí, J.M. and F. Ponti, *Si funciona, Cámbialo.* 2010, Barcelona: Gestión 2000.

www.ingramcontent.com/pod-product-compliance
Lightning Source LLC
Chambersburg PA
CBHW050529190326
41458CB00045B/6769/J